Edexcel GCSE
COMPUTER
SCIENCE

Steve Cushing

HODDER
EDUCATION
AN HACHETTE UK COMPANY

The Publishers would like to thank the following for permission to reproduce copyright material:

Photo credits: **page 12** Photodisc/Getty Images/ Business Today 35; **page 33** *left* Dirima/Fotolia, *right* Vladislav Kochelaevs/Fotolia; **page 89** bloomua/Fotolia; **page 118** Robert Gray; **page 127** istockphoto.com/Mark Evans (inset image Robert Gray); **page 167** Robert Gray; **page 170** Godfried Edelman/iStockPhoto.com; **page 179** Robert Gray; **page 183** Christian Jansky CC licence: http://creativecommons org/licenses/by-sa/3.0/; **page 192** Jwrodgers CC licence: http://creativecommons.org/licenses/by-sa/3.0/; **page 234** malajscy/Fotolia.

Every effort has been made to trace all copyright holders, but if any have been inadvertently overlooked the Publishers will be pleased to make the necessary arrangements at the first opportunity.

Hachette UK's policy is to use papers that are natural, renewable and recyclable products and made from wood grown in sustainable forests. The logging and manufacturing processes are expected to conform to the environmental regulations of the country of origin.

Orders: please contact Bookpoint Ltd, 130 Milton Park, Abingdon, Oxon OX14 4SB. Telephone: (44) 01235 827720. Fax: (44) 01235 400454. Lines are open 9.00–5.00 Monday to Saturday, with a 24-hour message answering service. Visit our website www.hoddereducation.com

First published in 2014 by
Hodder Education, an Hachette UK company,
338 Euston Road
London NW1 3BH

Impression number   5 4 3 2 1
Year   2017 2016 2015 2014

Cover photo by © arquiplay77 - Fotolia
Illustrations by Gray Publishing and Cartoon Studio
Typeset in ITC Garamond Light 11/16pt and produced by Gray Publishing, Tunbridge Wells
Printed in Italy

A catalogue record for this title is available from the British Library

ISBN 978 1 471 83735 7

Contents

Topic 1 Problem solving

Topic 2 Programming

Topic 3 Data

Topic 4 Computers

Contents

Topic 5 Communication and the internet

Topic 6 The bigger picture

Topic 1
PROBLEM SOLVING

1 Algorithms

Learning outcomes

- Understand what an algorithm is and what algorithms are used for, and be able to interpret algorithms.
- Be able to create an algorithm to solve a particular problem, making use of programming constructs and using an appropriate notation.
- Be able to describe the purpose of a given algorithm and explain how a simple algorithm works.
- Be able to identify the correct output of an algorithm for a given set of data.
- Be able to identify and correct errors in algorithms.
- Be able to code an algorithm into a high-level language.
- Understand how the choice of algorithm is influenced by the data structure and data values that need to be manipulated.
- Understand how standard algorithms work.

Language

As a programmer, it is essential that you understand the technical language and jargon associated with computer science. For many students, learning the computer jargon is probably the most frustrating part of any computer science course.

This textbook uses words that are obviously connected to the computer topic being covered and often represent concepts which don't exist in everyday vocabulary. This inevitably leads to a need to look up unfamiliar words in order to fully understand the concepts described.

What is an algorithm?

The word algorithm comes from the name al-Khwarizmi, a ninth-century Persian mathematician, who worked on 'written processes to achieve some goal'. Our word algebra comes from the term *al-jabr* that al-Khwarizmi introduced.

Algorithms are at the very heart of computer science. An algorithm is simply a set of steps that states how a task is performed. There are algorithms that you come across in everyday life, for example:

- cooking – *recipes*
- finding your way through a strange city – *directions*
- operating a washing machine – *instructions*
- playing music – *sheet music*.

Key term

An algorithm is simply a set of steps that defines how a task is performed.

Question

What is an algorithm?

A more scientific description of an algorithm would be: 'An algorithm is a finite sequence of step-by-step, discrete, unambiguous instructions for solving a particular problem.'

An algorithm has input data, and is expected to produce output data.

Each instruction in an algorithm should be carried out in a finite (*finite* is the opposite of infinite) amount of time in a deterministic way (*deterministic* means an algorithm, model, procedure, process, and so on, whose resulting behaviour is entirely determined by its initial state and inputs, not random). A deterministic algorithm is an algorithm which, given a particular input, will always produce the same output. The underlying code will always pass through the same sequence of states.

Since we can only input, store, process and output data on a computer, the instructions in our algorithms will be limited to these functions.

Before we can solve a problem, it must be understood.
■ Identify and name each of the inputs or givens.
■ Identify and name each of the outputs or results.
■ Assign a name to our algorithm (name).
■ Combine the previous three pieces of information into a formal statement (definition).
■ Results = name (givens).

Algorithms in maths

The study of algorithms does not depend on the existence of computers. Before we explore algorithms in code we need to understand how they work in mathematics. When the term algorithm is used in maths, it refers to a set of steps used to solve a mathematical problem. The steps for solving a long division problem are an algorithm, for example. If you are carrying out a long division for 53 divided by 3 you would have the following algorithm:
■ How many times does 3 go into 5? The answer is 1.
■ How many are left over? 2.
■ Put the 2 (20) in front of the 3.
■ How many times does 3 go into 23? The answer is 7 with a remainder of 2.
■ And, of course, the answer is 17 with a remainder of 2.

The step-by-step process used to do the long division is called a long division algorithm. Algorithms are used in mathematics often, especially in algebra.

Key point
Algorithms provide step-by-step methods of computation that a machine can carry out.

Algorithms in computing

We are interested in computer algorithms as these are fundamental to computer science. Most algorithms are not as simple or practical to apply manually as the one for long division. Most algorithms need computers because they would either take too much time for a person to apply, or involve so much detail as to make human error likely.

Algorithms provide the step-by-step methods (computation) that a machine can carry out. Having high-speed machines (computers) that can consistently follow and carry out a given set of instructions provides a reliable and effective means of solving problems. However, the computation that a given computer performs is only as good as the underlying algorithm used.

Every time you write a program you are creating an algorithm. You are creating a set of steps to perform a task. Knowledge of mathematical algorithms is essential as many computing algorithms follow the same processes. However, not all are the same. Let us look at some examples:

Mathematics	Computer science
The following instructions are the same in mathematics: A = B or B = A	But not in computer science, where: let A = B is different to let B = A
In mathematics we work with relations. A relation B = A + 1 means that it is true all the time	But in computer science, we work with assignments. We can have: A = 5 B = A + 1 A = 3 The relation B = A + 1 is true only after the second instruction and before the third one. After the third one, A = 3
The instruction A = A + 3 is false in mathematics. It cannot exist	But in computer science let A = A + 3 means the new value of A is equal to the old one plus 3
The instruction A + 6 = 3 is allowed in mathematics (it is an equation)	But let A + 6 = 3 has no meaning in computer science. The left side must be a variable so we would have to say 3 = A + 6

Understanding what can be effectively programmed and executed by computers, therefore, relies on the understanding of computer algorithms and mathematics. Algorithms solve general problems, not specific ones. Algorithms, therefore, are general computational methods used for solving particular problem instances.

Computers can execute instructions very quickly and reliably without error, so algorithms and computers are a perfect match.

Serial and parallel algorithms

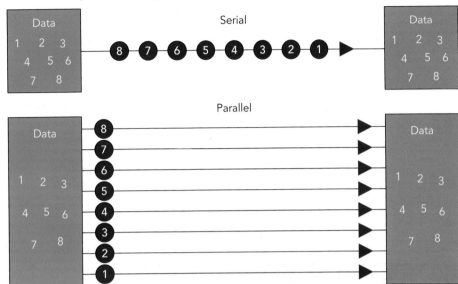

Serial and parallel algorithms work in different ways.

Serial

Parallel

Key terms

Serial algorithms are where each step or operation is carried out in a linear order.

Parallel algorithms are used with computers running parallel processors.

Sequence, selection and looping are three fundamental control structures used in programming.

Algorithms may also be divided into two different types:

- **Serial algorithms**: each step or operation is carried out in a linear order.
- **Parallel algorithms**: used with computers running parallel processors.

Solving problems

You need to be able to create an algorithm to solve problems, making use of programming constructs such as sequences, selection and repetition. To do that you will need to use an appropriate notation such as a flowchart, a written description or a program code.

Why design a program first?

To program correctly you will need to consider program design (planning) and the actual program coding. You can imagine what would happen if you built your house without first planning what you need and how it will be built. This type of planning is called 'control structured programming'.

There are three fundamental control structures:

- **sequence**
- **selection**
- **looping**.

A sequence control structure is simply a series of procedures that follow one another. A selection (if–then–else) control structure involves a choice.

Defining flow of control

Program flow control or flow of control can be defined as the order in which a program is executed (carried out) or evaluated. There are three different flow control structures that every programming language supports. However, different programming languages may support different kinds of control flow statements.

Why it is an advantage to have structured programs?

There are several advantages of a structured approach when designing coded solutions. One advantage is that a structured approach reduces the complexity of programming, as **modularity** allows the programmer to tackle problems in a logical fashion. Also, using logical structures when designing programs ensures clarity within the flow of the control of the code.

Another advantage is that structured programming increases the productivity as a consequence of the modular approach. This allows more than one programmer to work on a project at the same time.

Since modules can be reused, it saves time and reduces complexity, as well as increasing reliability. It also offers an easier method to update or fix the program by replacing individual modules rather than replacing larger amounts of code.

Structured programming makes extensive use of what are called subroutines, block structures and *for* and *while* loops. This approach is in contrast to using simple tests and jumps such as using the *goto* statement that would eventually lead to something that is often referred to as 'spaghetti code', that is disorganised, unstructured code which is very difficult to follow. We will explore all of these later in the book.

Structures: how things are broken down

As we have seen at a basic level, structured programs are comprised of a simple, hierarchical flow. If we break down a problem into modules or blocks, we can examine the necessary structures. These will consist entirely of three types of logic structures.

We will explore the elements of a simple program to work out the number of calories a person actually eats and the number of calories that this person should be eating. The program will show the difference.

We will need the test subject to input his or her details. The flowchart shows an example of the tasks we could identify before writing any code.

Key term

Modularity is breaking a task down into smaller modules.

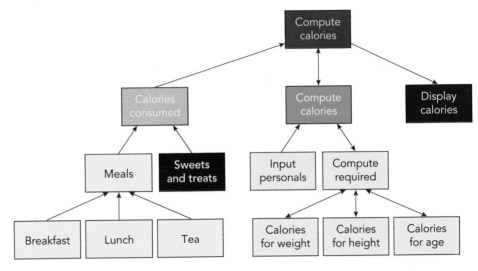

Our calorie-counter program as a flowchart.

The following three basic constructs for flow of control will be sufficient for our task; indeed, they are sufficient to implement any 'proper' algorithm:

- Sequence: a *sequence* is a linear progression where one task is performed sequentially after another.
- Selection: *if–then–else* is a decision (selection) in which a choice is made between two alternative courses of action.
- Iteration: *while* is a loop (repetition) with a simple conditional test at its beginning.

Although these constructs are sufficient, it is often useful to include three further constructs:

- *Repeat–until* is a loop with a simple conditional test at the end.
- *Case* is a multiway branch (decision) based on the value of an expression. *Case* is a generalisation of *if–then–else*.
- *For* is a 'counting' loop.

Before we look at these logic structures in more detail, there are three main ways of representing them: code, pseudocode and flowcharts.

Why use anything but code?

The very basic building block of any coded solution is a simple section of straight-line code with no programming routes leaving the program statement, and only one route entering it from the code that came before it.

When the syntax of a programming language encloses structures between bracketed keywords such as an *if* statement or a code section bracketed by *Begin … End*, the language is referred to as *block-structured*.

Question

Briefly describe the following constructs:
- sequence
- selection
- iteration.

It is possible to write structured programming in any programming language; however, it is preferable to use a procedural coding language.

Historically, the languages that were first used for structured programming were ALGOL, Pascal and Ada. Nowadays, most programming languages include features that encourage a structured approach to coding and actually deliberately leave out other features in an attempt to prevent the language being used for unstructured coding.

Solutions to simple programming exercises can often be designed and implemented by just sitting down and writing code. It is, however, extremely difficult to write solutions to complex problems using this approach and impossible to debug. For these reasons a structured design process is preferred.

There are many methods of structurally designing programs and these have the following advantages:

- The modular design allows for improved testing.
- They allow early discovery of design errors.
- They allow for large problems to be broken down into smaller, more manageable sections.
- They allow for programs that can be modified easily.
- They encourage documentation that is thorough and has clarity.

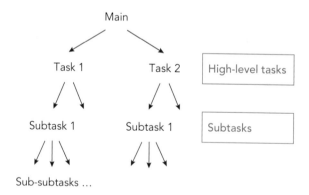

A flowchart showing a structural design.

Applying structural design methods to programming makes it far more likely that the program will run successfully with the minimum amount of time and effort spent building it. Structural design methods increase the possibility of finding design mistakes early on in the design process and, consequently, this greatly reduces the cost of repairing any errors.

Structured design methodology also allows for the modification of programs at a later date. These design techniques allow changes to be

Question

Why would a computer programmer want to use a flowchart during a design process?

completed far more easily and efficiently as they offer a much clearer and more complete procedure when producing supporting documentation.

Structured designs also offer the ability for them to be broken down into natural modules, which improves testing and offers the opportunity for multiple design teams to work on areas of a project with the reassurance that the completed programs will be compatible with one another.

Top-down design

The best way to approach the design of a program is to use top-down design. To do this you first map out the entire program and then identify the major components that it will require and the tasks to be performed.

The programmer can then use flowcharts and general statements to represent the logical flow of the program. Once the major tasks have been identified, the programmer can focus on each separate task in greater detail.

Basic structures

A structured process is one where all of the processes and decisions must fit into one of three basic structured elements: *sequence*, *selection* and *iteration*. You should make sure that you understand that each of the structures always has exactly one input and one output. This means that a single process block can represent the structure itself.

Key term

The **sequence process** is just a series of processes that operate one after the other, *if–then–else*.

The **sequence process** is just a series of processes that operate one after the other. Most program solutions are represented at the highest level by a *sequence*, possibly with a loop from the *end* symbol back to the *start* symbol.

Sequence   Selection
(if … then … else)   Iteration
(while)

Sequence, selection and iteration flowcharts.

The *selection* or *if–then–else* process logically completes the Boolean decision block by providing two separate processes. One of the processes will be carried out in each path from the Boolean decision.

The *iteration* or *while* procedure allows for a conditional loop structure to be represented within a program. The decision to execute the process in the loop is made before the first execution of the process.

Using pseudocode

Pseudocode consists of natural language-like statements that precisely describe the steps of an algorithm or program.

Pseudocode must have the following features:

- It should contain statements that describe actions.
- It should focus on the logic of the algorithm or program.
- It should avoid language-specific elements.
- It should be written at a level so that the desired programming code can be generated almost automatically from each statement.
- It should contain steps. Subordinate numbers and/or indentation are used for dependent statements in selection and repetition structures.

Common action keywords

Several keywords are often used to indicate common input, output and processing operations:

- Input: READ, OBTAIN, GET.
- Output: PRINT, DISPLAY, SHOW.
- Compute: COMPUTE, CALCULATE, DETERMINE.
- Initialise: SET, INIT.
- Add one: INCREMENT, BUMP.

Using flowcharts

There are many different design procedures and techniques for building large software projects. Such large projects might include developing a new database for a large organisation. The technique discussed here, however, is for smaller coding projects and is referred to as 'top-down, structured flowchart methodology'.

Basic elements of flowcharts

The flowchart symbols denoting the basic building blocks of structural programming are shown in the diagram.

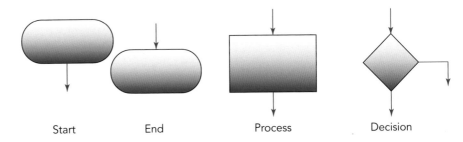

Start   End   Process   Decision

Flowchart symbols for start, end, process and decision.

The *start* symbol obviously represents the start of a process. It always has exactly one output. The *start* symbol is labelled with a brief description of the process carried out by the flowchart. The *end* symbol represents the end of a process. It always has exactly one input and generally contains either *end* or *return* depending on its function in the overall process of the flowchart.

A *process* symbol is representative of some operation that is carried out on an element of data. It usually contains a brief explanation describing the process being carried out on the data. It is possible that the process could even be further broken down into simpler steps by another complete flowchart representing that process. If this is the case, the flowchart that represents the process will have the same label in the *start* symbol as the description in the process symbol at the higher level. A process always has exactly one input and one output.

A **decision symbol** always makes a Boolean choice. The label in a *decision* symbol should be a question that clearly has only two possible answers. The *decision* symbol will have exactly one input and two outputs. The two outputs will be labelled with the two answers to the question in order to show the direction of the logic flow depending on the decision made.

On-page and off-page *connectors* may also appear in some flowcharts. For the purpose of this chapter we will restrict ourselves to flowcharts that can be represented on a single page.

Here are some general rules for flowcharts:
- All the flowchart symbols are connected by flow lines (must be arrows not lines).

Key term

A decision symbol always makes a Boolean choice.

- Flow lines enter the top of the symbol and exit from the bottom, except for the *decision* symbol, which can have flow lines exiting from the bottom or the sides.
- Flowcharts are drawn so that flow generally goes from top to bottom.
- The beginning and the end of the flowchart are indicated using the *terminal* symbol.

Using flowcharts or pseudocode to represent a programming sequence

Sequence

A **sequence** is where a set of instructions or actions is ordered, meaning that each action follows the previous action.

A simple sequence of actions.

An example of a sequence in the real world could be:
- brush teeth
- wash face
- comb hair
- smile in mirror.

As you can see, sequences are a useful tool for showing what happens and in what order.

Selection

In practice, sequences are not a simple line: the next action usually depends on the last decision. This is called selection. In selection one statement within a set of program statements is executed depending on the state of the program at that instance.

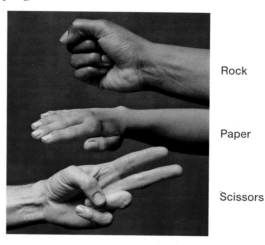

Rock, paper, scissors game. A looping structure.

Key term

A sequence is where a set of instructions or actions is ordered, meaning that each action follows the previous action.

Task

Produce a sequence to show how to brush your teeth.

First, let's explore programming in terms of what is called a conditional sequence. The problem we will look at is the rock, paper, scissors game.

If the first player is a rock and the second player is scissors, the first player wins, but *if* the second player is paper *then* they win.

This game leads to one outcome or sequence of events to be executed if a statement was true, and another outcome or sequence of events to be triggered if the statement was false.

Task

Produce a looping sequence to show the game rock, paper, scissors where the winner of each game scores one point and the overall winner is the best of 21 points.

Task

Design a simple rock, paper, scissors game in Python or your chosen language.

In most programming languages, selection structures take the form *if–then–else*. Our game also contains repetitions: when the game has finished it starts again. Another name for this is a looping structure (a list of instructions to do more than once). You write this type of program to make the computer repeat a certain command or sequence of commands. The loop may run for a predetermined number of times, until a certain condition becomes true, or as long as a certain condition remains true. You could tell the computer to:

- Do the following 20 times.
- Do the following once for each word in the list.
- Repeat the following until the user carries out a particular action.

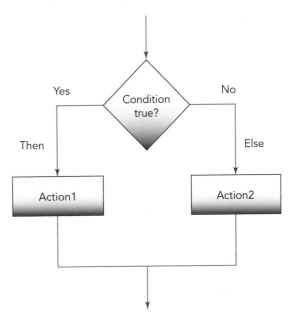

A flowchart representing selection.

Selections are usually expressed as 'decision' keywords such as *if–then–else–endif*, *switch* or *case*. They are at the heart of all programming.

If we explore what this might look like using pseudocode:

```
if condition is true
    then
  perform instructions in Action1
    else
  perform instructions in Action2
endif
```

or

```
IF condition THEN
   sequence 1
ELSE
   sequence 2
ENDIF
```

or, for example, if a student's mark in a Computer Science exam is greater than or equal to 60:

```
   Print "passed"
else
   Print "failed"
```

A coded example of this in Python could be:

```
if name == 'Steve':
   print('You have such a cool name!')
else:
   print('Not a bad name, but the coolest name is Steve.')
```

So we have two options. If the entered name is 'Steve' the program prints one string, if it is anything else it prints a second string.

Task

Produce a simple coded solution in your chosen programming language for a user to input his or her name and for a simple message to be printed using the data entered.

Derived structures

As has already been suggested, flowcharts and pseudocode can be represented by basic structures; however, on occasions it is useful to use some additional structures, each of which can themselves be constructed from the above structures. These *derived structures* are shown in the following diagram.

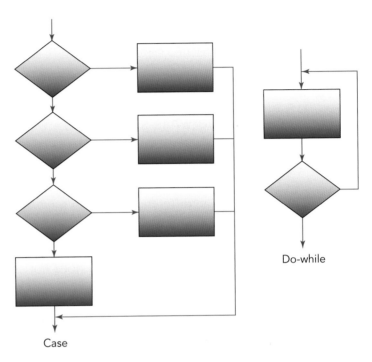

The derived structures *case* and *do-while* for use in a flowchart.

As you can see, the *do-while* structure is different from the *while* structure because the process contained within the loop always executes at least once. This procedure is the same as if the process was performed once before going into a *while* loop. In the *while* structure it is possible that the process may never be executed. You should understand that although the *while* structure is often used, the *do-while* structure is sometimes used because it is more intuitive. Choosing between the two is difficult so let's look at a few rules:

- Are you repeating or copying/pasting code you have already used?
- Which way uses fewer lines of code? Normally less is better.
- There are times when using more lines of code is more efficient but you should never repeat yourself when coding.

Key point

Use a while loop only to loop forever, and that means probably never. This only applies to Python; other languages are different. Use a for loop for all other kinds of looping, especially if there is a fixed or limited number of things to loop over.

Task

Produce a do-while flowchart to show how to make a breakfast of tea and toast.

Now let's look in more detail at code and how it can be represented.

While statements

While statements are efficient loops that will continue to loop until the condition is false.

```
WHILE condition
    sequence
ENDWHILE
```

Do-while statements

Do-while statements are also efficient loops that will continue to loop until the condition is false.

The difference between a *while* loop and a *do-while* loop is that in a *while* loop the condition is checked before the first iteration of the loop and in a *do-while* the condition is checked at the end of the loop. Here is a simple example; obviously 5 does not equal 8 so the condition is false:

```
while (5 == 8)
    // this code will never run
do
    // this code will run once
while (5 == 8)
```

The case study structure

The *case* structure is useful in representing a series of *selection (if–then–else)* procedures where there are more than two *decisions* to be made. Hence, the *decision* symbols are identical except for the choice being compared. For example, the *decision* could be 'is the make of the car … ?' Each *decision* block would then have a different make of car as the choice. One aspect of this structure that you should acknowledge is that the *true* result always flows to the right, with the *false* result flowing into the next *decision* symbol, and also there will always be one less *decision* symbol than the number of choices.

The diagram illustrates an example of a properly and an improperly structured flowchart. The unstructured flowchart demonstrates what can happen if a program is written first and then a flowchart is created to represent the program. As was mentioned earlier in this chapter, this type of unstructured flow is referred to as 'spaghetti coding' and normally has aspects of its structure impossibly intertwined around other elements. It should be realised that a programming solution of this nature is very difficult to understand, implement, debug and maintain.

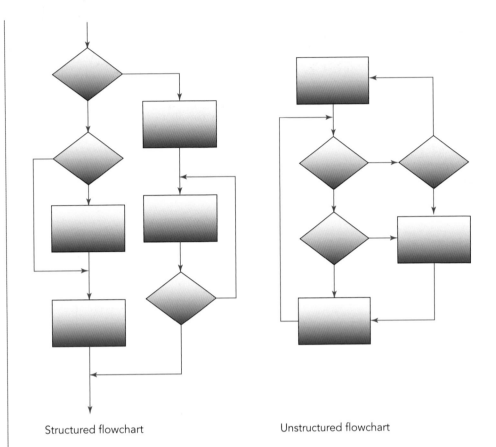

Structured flowchart   Unstructured flowchart

Properly and improperly structured flowcharts.

Question

Write a program flowchart for a game that does the following.

- It assigns the value called *outcome* to a variable called *guessanswer*.
- It then assigns user input to another variable called *guess1*.
- If the user enters the value 'Computer' then the program outputs 'winner', otherwise it outputs 'incorrect' and allows the user to have another guess.
- It allows the game to continue until the user guesses correctly.

Task

Produce a structured flowchart to show how to make a cup of tea. Remember that some tasks can happen while other things are happening, so you should end up with a structured flowchart with decision symbols (for example, you cannot add water to the teapot until the water has been boiled).

Looping/iteration and derived structures in more detail

Iteration is where a statement is executed in a loop until the program reaches a certain state or the intended operations have been applied to every data element of an array. If you look at the following diagram you can see that the iteration/loop keeps on occurring until a false statement is reached.

In programming, iterations are usually expressed as loop keywords such as *while, repeat, for* or *do … until*. Again we can show this using a flowchart.

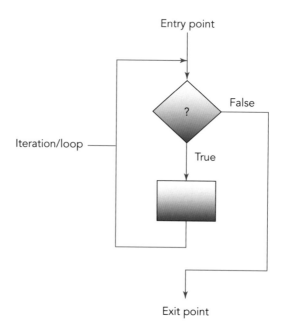

A flowchart showing an iteration/loop.

It is sometimes recommended that each iteration (loop) should have only one entry point and one exit point, and a few programming languages actually enforce this. Let's look at an example.

Task

Create a flowchart to show how to take a bath or shower. Start from arriving in the bathroom fully dressed and end when you are dressed again. You can start with a simple sequence but you must then add conditional loops.

Question

Complete the instructions on the following flowchart by adding notes on how to play the game of snakes and ladders.

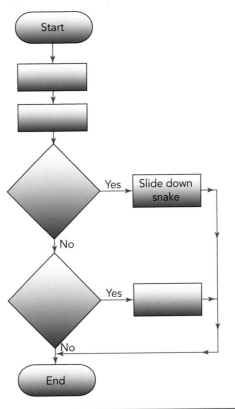

Task

Write the sequence complete with loops and conditional statements for the game of rock, paper, scissors.

Let's say you wanted a string printed 100 times. By using a loop statement you do not have to code the print statement 100 times, you simply tell the computer to display a string that number of times.

In Python, the loop statement can be written as follows:

```
count = 0
while count < 100:
    print("Computer Science is great fun!")
    count = count + 1
```

So what is happening here? Let's look at a simple flowchart.

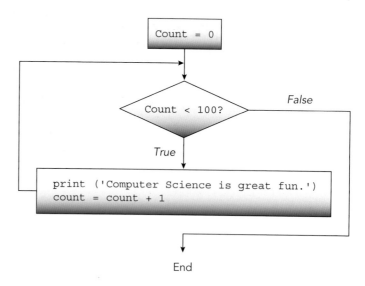

Flowchart to show how to print a string of text 100 times.

So while the count is less than 100, the program will continue to print. Once the program reaches 100 it will stop.

We can also loop with user input. The following Python code creates a simple guess the number game.

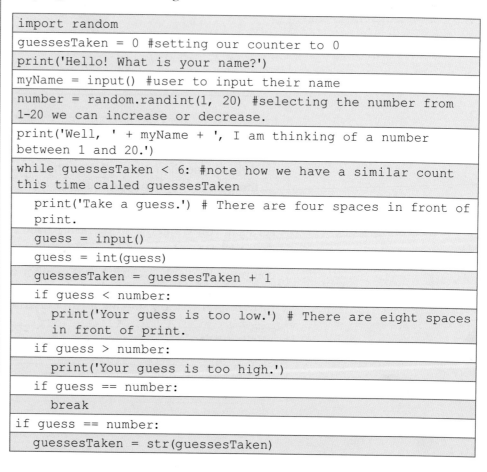

```python
import random
guessesTaken = 0 #setting our counter to 0
print('Hello! What is your name?')
myName = input() #user to input their name
number = random.randint(1, 20) #selecting the number from 1-20 we can increase or decrease.
print('Well, ' + myName + ', I am thinking of a number between 1 and 20.')
while guessesTaken < 6: #note how we have a similar count this time called guessesTaken
    print('Take a guess.') # There are four spaces in front of print.
    guess = input()
    guess = int(guess)
    guessesTaken = guessesTaken + 1
    if guess < number:
        print('Your guess is too low.') # There are eight spaces in front of print.
    if guess > number:
        print('Your guess is too high.')
    if guess == number:
        break
if guess == number:
    guessesTaken = str(guessesTaken)
```

```
print('Good job, ' + myName + '! You guessed my number in
   ' + guessesTaken + ' guesses!')
if guess != number:
   number = str(number)
   print('Nope. The number I was thinking of was ' + number)
```

As you can see, *while* loops and *if* statements are an essential part of programming. A *while statement* is called an iterative control statement as it repeatedly executes a set of statements that are based on a Boolean expression or condition.

As long as the condition of a *while* statement is true, the statements within the loop are (re-)executed. Once the condition becomes false, the iteration ends and control continues with the first statement after the *while* loop.

Nested loops

Nested loops consist of an outer loop and one or more inner loops. Each time the outer loop is repeated, the inner loops are re-entered and started again as if new. The diagram shows a simple example.

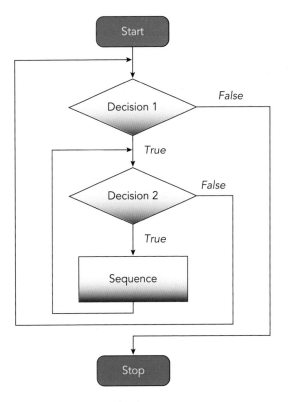

A flowchart showing a nested loop.

Key term

Nested loops have an outer loop and one or more inner loops. Each time the outer loop repeats, the inner loops are re-entered and start again as if new.

Let's look at an example of a nested loop. First, we need a few students:

```
students = [("Sally", ["CompSci", "Physics"]),
            ("Robert", ["Art", "CompSci", "Stats"]),
            ("Charlotte", ["CompSci", "French",
            "Economics"]),
            ("Steve", ["CompSci", "French", "Economics",
            "CommLaw"]),
            ("Carole", ["Sociology", "French", "Law",
            "Stats", "Music"])]
```

So we have assigned a list of five elements to a variable called students.

Now let's print out each student name and the number of subjects they are enrolled for:

```
# print all students with a count of their courses.
for (name, subjects) in students:
    print(name, "takes", len(subjects), "courses")
```

Python would give us the following output:

```
Sally takes 2 courses
Robert takes 3 courses
Charlotte takes 3 courses
Steve takes 4 courses
Carole takes 5 courses
```

Let's say we want to ask how many students are taking a Computer Science course ("CompSci"). This needs a counter, and for each student we need a second embedded loop that tests each of the subjects in turn:

```
# Count how many students are taking CompSci
counter = 0
for (name, subjects) in students:
    for s in subjects:          # a nested loop!
        if s == "CompSci":
            counter += 1
print("The number of students taking CompSci is", counter)
```

The output will be:

```
The number of students taking CompSci is 4
```

As the code gets more complicated, you will see how important it is to work out what we need before starting to program. These basic flowchart symbols and pseudocode are the building blocks needed to express any desired logic in the form of a computer program.

Question

What is a variable?

Key point

By using flowcharts or pseudocode it is possible to describe easily the purpose of a given algorithm and explain how a simple algorithm works.

Question

Write a program in pseudocode to take seven input values and to output the following:

- the total value
- the highest value
- the lowest value
- the average.

Speeding up an algorithm

There are some very common problems that we can use computers to solve. These problems include the following:

- Searching through many records for a specific record or set of records.
- Placing records in order. This is called sorting.

There are many algorithms available to perform searches and sorts.

A question you should always ask when selecting a search algorithm is 'How fast does the search have to be?' The reason is that, in general, the faster the algorithm is, the more complex it is.

You don't always need to use or should use the fastest algorithm. If speed is important it will change your decision about how to write the algorithm.

Search algorithms

Binary search

Let's look at the following algorithm:

```
Get the search criterion (key)
Get the first record from the file
While ( (record < key) and (still more records) )
   Get the next record
End _ while
If ( record = key )
   Then success
   Else there is no match in the file
End _ else
```

When do we know that there wasn't a record in the file that matched the key?

Let's do a comparison between a sorted and an unsorted list.

If the order was ascending alphabetical on last names, how would the search for Anthony Adams on the ordered list compare with the search on the unordered list?

Unordered list	Ordered list
If Anthony Adams was in the list?	If Anthony Adams was in the list?
If Anthony Adams was not in the list?	If Anthony Adams was not in the list?

How about in the case of Xian Xui?

Unordered list	Ordered list
If Xian Xui was in the list?	If Xian Xui was in the list?
If Xian Xui was not in the list?	If Xian Xui was not in the list?

Key point

The search is faster on an ordered list only when the item being searched for is not in the list.

The search is faster on an ordered list only when the item being searched for is not in the list. Also, the list has to first be placed in order for the ordered search. Because of this the efficiency of the algorithms is roughly the same.

If we need a faster search we will require a completely different algorithm.

If we have an ordered list and we know how many things are in the list (that is the number of records in a file), we can use a different strategy.

Binary search gets its name because the algorithm continually divides the list into two parts. It looks at the centre value and disregards anything below or above what we are trying to find. Let's say we are looking for item 6 from nine ordered items.

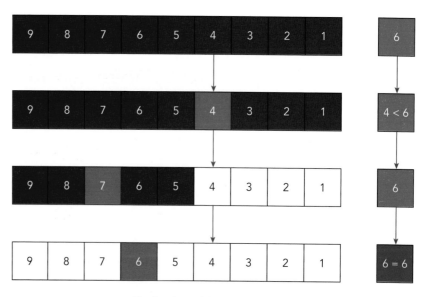

Finding item 6 from nine items.

So each time you get to discard half of the remaining list and as such a binary search is a very fast search algorithm on sorted lists. But the list has to be sorted before we can search it with binary search. To be really efficient we also need a fast sort algorithm.

There are a number of sort algorithms:

- bubble sort
- selection sort
- insertion sort
- heap sort
- merge sort
- quick sort.

Bubble sort is the slowest. Quick sort is the fastest.

As with searching, the faster the sorting algorithm, the more complex it tends to be.

Bubble sort

The simplest sorting algorithm is bubble sort.

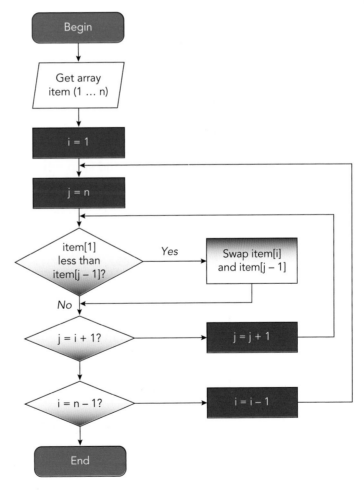

A flowchart showing a bubble sort algorithm.

The bubble sort works by iterating down an array to be sorted from the first element to the last, comparing each pair of elements and switching their positions if necessary.

This process is repeated as many times as necessary until all of the array is sorted correctly.

The worst case scenario is that the array is in reverse order, and that the first element in a sorted array is the last element in the starting array. But even then the maximum number of exchanges that will be needed will be equal to the length of the array.

Selection sort

The idea of a selection sort is a simple process. It works by repeatedly finding the next largest (or smallest) element in the array. It then moves the element to its final position in the sorted array.

Let's assume that we wish to sort the array in increasing order, that is with the smallest element at the beginning of the array and the largest element at the end. First, we need to select the largest element and move it to the highest index position. This is done by swapping the element at the highest index with the largest element. This reduces the effective size of the array by one element and then repeats the process on the new smaller array, called a sub-array.

The process would stop when the effective size of the array becomes one. This is because an array of one element is already sorted as there is nothing bigger or smaller than it. For example, consider the following array, shown with array elements in sequence separated by commas:

```
43, 52, 2, 89, 23, 56
```

The largest number is 89 and the smallest 2. The left-most element is at index zero, and the right-most element is at the highest array index, in our case 5 (the effective size of our array is 6).

The largest element in this effective array (index 0–5) is at index 3. We then swap the element at index 3 with that at index 5.

The result is:

```
43, 52, 2, 56, 23, 89
```

We reduce the effective size of the array to 5, making the highest index in the effective array now 4.

Key point

Bubble sort is the simplest sorting algorithm.

The largest element in this effective array (index 0–4) is at index 4, so we swap elements at index 3 and 4 (in bold type):

```
43, 52, 2, 23, 56, 89
```

If we repeat this three times we will have:

```
2, 23, 43, 52, 56, 89
```

The data is now sorted.

Depth and breadth search algorithms

In some situations it is necessary to alter the order of a search in order to make the search more efficient. To explore this we need to understand data trees and nodes. We will look at nodes later in the book. For now, to see what this might mean, here are two alternative methods of searching a data tree.

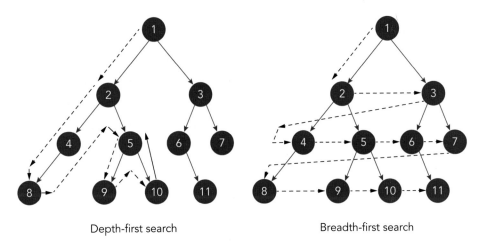

Depth-first search   Breadth-first search

Depth-first and breadth-first searches are two alternative methods of searching a data tree.

Depth-first searches begin by diving down as quickly as possible. Breadth-first searches traverse the tree or graph level by level.

Data structure and algorithms

As part of your course you will need to develop an understanding of data structures and algorithms. These are fundamental to computer science and software engineering.

The performance of software is strongly influenced by:

- The choice of appropriate data structures for storing the software's data in order to effectively store, manipulate and retrieve the data values.
- The use of algorithms that are appropriate and efficient across the various layers of system implementation.

Minimum and maximum

Sometimes a user will want to find the minimum and maximum in a defined list. If we explore a small program that allows a user to type in a list of numbers and then from this list calculate the minimum and maximum, an algorithm would be required. To make the algorithm a little simpler, we will ask the user to enter a count of the numbers in the list before entering the actual numbers.

The algorithm for this might be:

initialise
get count of numbers
enter numbers and find maximum and minimum
output results

Of course, the user may enter any number of numbers, even no numbers. This may seem a bit stupid but it is not uncommon when writing a general-purpose function to allow for the possibility of null input. Let's modify our algorithm to accept this possibility.

initialise
get count of numbers
if count is zero
then exit
otherwise {
enter numbers and find maximum
and minimum
output results
}

In our new algorithm, once the count of the numbers is known, a loop is executed that number of times, each time reading in a number and somehow using that number to find the maximum and minimum. In this loop, the number of times the loop is executed is known: it is equal to the count of the numbers.

loop n times
{
body of loop.
}

Algorithms often repeat a set of instructions a set number of times. Note that braces have been used to make the body of the loop into a compound statement. Each time the loop is executed it is the instructions between the braces that are executed.

We now have the following new version of the algorithm:

```
initialise
get count of numbers
if count is zero
  then exit
  otherwise {
    loop count times
    {
    enter a number
    process the number
    }
    output results
    }
```

We now need to compute the maximum and minimum values. We will use the phrase 'process the number'. If you wanted to do this manually, one way would be to start at the beginning of the list and work through the list systematically, always remembering the smallest number seen so far. Whenever a number is found that is smaller than the memorised number, the memorised number would be replaced by the new smaller number. At the start of the list the smallest number yet seen is of course the first number, and when the end of the list is reached the memorised number is the smallest. We could do the same thing for the largest number. This leads to the following algorithm:

```
get count of numbers
if count is zero
  then exit
  otherwise {
    get first number
    set small to number
    set large to number
    loop count-1 times
    {
      enter a number
      if number is less than small
        then set small to number
      if number is greater than large
        then set large to number
    }
    print small and large
    }
```

We can now check this algorithm by doing a simple desk check with the following data, for example:

count = 5
numbers are 3 6 1 9 2

The different values taken during the algorithm would be as follows:

-	-	-	-	begin
6	-	-	-	enter count
6	3	3	3	enter first number
6	6	6	3	first loop execution
6	1	6	1	second loop execution
6	9	9	1	third loop execution
6	2	9	1	final loop execution

Finding the mathematical mean

Let's assume that we have N numbers and want to find their arithmetic mean. The simplest method is to sum all values and divide by the number of values:

```
def simple_mean(array[N]): # pseudocode
    sum = 0
    for i = 1 to N
        sum += array[i]
    return sum / N
```

This will work well but it does require large integers.

Another method could be:

```
sum = 0
rest = 0
for num in numbers:
    sum += num / N
    rest += num % N
    sum += rest / N
    rest = rest % N
return sum, rest
```

Count algorithms

Count algorithms (often referred to as a *countSort*) are important as they allow us to examine large data streams for patterns. This is particularly useful in the fields of data compression, sight and sound recognition, and other artificial intelligence applications.

Let's look at a simple count algorithm:

```
function countingSort(array, min, max):
    count: array of (max - min + 1) elements
    initialise count with 0
    for each number in array do
        count[number - min] := count[number - min] + 1
    done
    z := 0
    for i from min to max do
        while ( count[i - min] > 0 ) do
            array[z] := i
            z := z+1
            count[i - min] := count[i - min] - 1
        done
    done
```

Algorithm efficiency

Some algorithms are more efficient than others. It is obviously better to have an efficient algorithm. There are two main measures of the efficiency of an algorithm: *time* and *space*.

The 'time measure' is a function that describes the amount of time an algorithm takes, with an output of the amount of data input to the algorithm. In this sense 'time' can mean a number of things including the number of memory accesses performed, the number of times an inner loop is executed, the number of comparisons between integers or any other natural unit related to the amount of real time the algorithm will take.

A 'space measure' is a different function that describes the amount of memory (space) an algorithm takes in terms of the amount of input to the algorithm. People often speak of 'extra' memory that is needed, but this does not include the memory needed to store the input itself.

Key point

Some algorithms can be more efficient than other algorithms. Always use the most efficient algorithm.

2 Decomposition

Learning outcomes

- Be able to analyse a problem, investigate requirements and design solutions.
- Be able to decompose a problem into smaller sub-problems.

Key term

Decomposition is a general approach to solving a problem by breaking it up into smaller problems then solving it one problem at a time.

Decomposition is a general approach to solving a problem by breaking it up into smaller tasks and solving each of the smaller tasks separately, either in parallel or one problem at a time (sequentially).

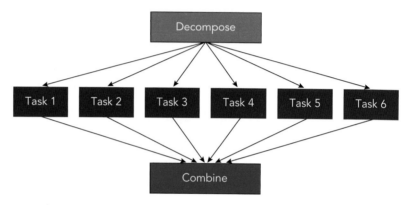

Decomposition of a problem into tasks allows programmers to deal with the sub-problems before combining them to solve the original problem.

In decomposition the programmer decomposes (breaks down) the task so that:

- Each sub-problem task can be solved independently.
- Each sub-problem task is at (roughly) the same level of detail.
- The solutions to the sub-problems can be combined to solve the original problem.

The advantages of the decomposition approach are as follows:

- Different people can work on different sub-problem tasks at the same time.
- Maintenance is easier.
- Parallelisation may be possible.

The disadvantages of the decomposition approach are as follows:

- Poorly understood problems are hard to decompose.
- The solutions to the sub-problem tasks might not combine to solve the original problem.

When decomposition is done sequentially, the advantage comes from the fact that problem complexity grows more than linearly.

As an example let's look at a simple non-computing task: making breakfast.

For breakfast you might have a cup of coffee and a slice of toast with butter and jam. You could do just one task at a time, but in reality you will break the job into two parts: making the toast and jam; and making the coffee. You will now produce the two component parts in parallel, using the time while the kettle boils to butter the toast. This is an example of decomposition into smaller tasks and is fundamental to computer science.

Other examples of decomposition

When a chef writes down a recipe for a meal, they are creating an algorithm that others can follow to replicate that meal. Each part of the recipe is listed separately, the overall meal is decomposed into separate dishes, and these are often decomposed further. For example, when preparing an apple pie there is making the pastry and preparing the filling.

When a football manager thinks about tactics for a particular game he is designing a set of algorithms for his players to follow during the match. Each player has his own set of instructions.

Abstraction is another important concept to understand.

When someone drives a car, they change gears, turn corners and apply the brakes. They know that the gearstick changes the gears, the steering wheel turns the front wheels and the brake lever applies the brakes, but they may not know all the mechanics of how these systems work.

It is possible to learn how to drive a car without knowing how all the components work.

Abstraction is used to manage complexity. Software developers use abstraction to decompose complex systems into smaller components.

In mathematics, if we are working out a complicated problem, one abstraction in order to solve the overall problem might be to add and subtract fractions with different denominators (bottom line of a fraction). We follow an abstracted algorithm. For example, if we wanted to work out $\frac{5}{6} - \frac{3}{4}$:

- The common denominator of 6 and 4 is 12 (6 goes into 12 two times; 4 goes into 12 three times).
- The problem then becomes $\frac{5}{6} = \frac{10}{12}$ (multiplying two times) and $\frac{3}{4} = \frac{9}{12}$ (multiplying three times).
- $\frac{10}{12} - \frac{9}{12} = \frac{1}{12}$.

Problem solving

At the heart of computational problem solving are two essential points:
- a representation that captures all the relevant aspects of the problem
- an algorithm that solves the problem by use of the representation.

Let's consider a problem.

Fred wants to cross the river.

A man called Fred wishes to cross a 10-metre wide river with a wolf, a white goat and a bale of freshly cut hay. He has a small blue boat and oars, but unfortunately, he can only take one thing across the river at a time. The problem is, if he leaves the wolf and the goat alone together the wolf will eat the goat, and if he leaves the goat with the hay, the goat will eat the hay. They are together on bank B. How does he do it?

There is a simple algorithmic approach for solving this problem.

You could simply try all possible combinations of items that may be rowed back and forth across the river. Trying all possible solutions to a given problem is referred to as a brute-force approach.

Representing the problem

Only the relevant aspects of the river-crossing problem need to be represented. All the irrelevant details can be ignored. A representation that leaves out details of what is being represented is a form of abstraction.

- Is the colour of the boat relevant?
- Is the man's name relevant?
- Is the width of the river relevant?

The short answer to each of these is no, the only relevant information is where each item is at each step. The collective location of each item, in this case, refers to the state of the problem. If we start with:

- goat = G
- hay = H
- man = M
- river banks are A and B
- wolf = W,

then we have:

A		B
		G H W M

We need to end up with:

A		B
G H W M		

Each step we show needs to correspond to the man rowing a particular object across the river (or the man rowing alone).

Let's look at the first step:

A		B
G M		H W

The man (M) has taken the goat (G) to the other side of the river.

Task

1. Solve the rest of the river-crossing problem.
2. Develop or find an existing algorithm for computationally solving the problem using this representation.

Topic 2
PROGRAMMING

3 Developing code

Learning outcomes

- Be able to write programs in a high-level programming language.
- Understand the benefit of producing programs that are easy to read, and be able to use techniques to improve readability and to explain how the code works.
- Be able to differentiate between types of error in programs.
- Be able to design and use test plans and test data.
- Be able to interpret error messages and identify, locate and fix errors in a program.
- Be able to identify what value a variable will hold at a given point in a program.
- Be able to make effective use of tools offered in an integrated development environment.
- Be able to evaluate the strengths and weaknesses of a program and suggest improvements.
- Be able to work safely, respectfully, responsibly and securely when using computers.

High-level programming languages

Programming languages known as **high-level programming languages** were developed mainly in the 1950s. In your Computer Science course you must be able to program in one of the following high-level languages: Python, Java or C.

High-level programming languages are platform independent, which means that you can write a program in a high-level language and run it on different types of machines and operating systems.

High-level programming languages are easy to learn as they use English-like code. The instructions in a high-level programming language are called statements.

Here, for example, is a high-level language statement that 'computes' the area of a circle with a radius of 10 using the value of pi (π) as 3.1415. (The area of a circle is calculated as the radius squared times π.)

```
area = 10 * 10 * 3.1415
```

There are many high-level programming languages, and each was designed for a specific purpose. Here is a list of some popular ones.

Key term

High-level programming languages are languages that resemble a natural language. Each instruction translates into many machine instructions.

Key point

High-level programming languages are platform independent: programs can be run on different types of machines and operating systems.

Question

What is a high-level programming language?

Language	Description
BASIC	Beginner's All-purpose Symbolic Instruction Code. It was designed to be learned and used easily by beginners
C	Developed at Bell Laboratories, USA. C combines the power of an assembly language with the ease of use and portability of a high-level language
C++	C++ is an object-oriented language, based on C
C#	Pronounced C sharp. It is a hybrid of Java and C++ and was developed by Microsoft, USA
COBOL	COmmon Business Oriented Language. Used for business applications
FORTRAN	FORmula TRANslation. Popular for scientific and mathematical applications
Java	Developed by Sun Microsystems, now part of Oracle, USA. It is widely used for developing platform-independent internet applications
Pascal	Named after French mathematician Blaise Pascal (1623–62), who pioneered calculating machines in the seventeenth century. It is a simple, structured, general-purpose language primarily for teaching programming
Python	A simple general-purpose scripting language good for writing short programs

Question

Describe the main benefits to a programmer of using a high-level programming language.

A program written in any high-level programming language is called a source program or source code. Computers cannot understand a source program, however, and because of this a source program must be translated into machine code for execution. The translation can be done using another programming tool called an interpreter or a compiler.

Interpreter

An interpreter reads one statement from the source code, translates it to the machine code or virtual machine code, and then executes it. The following diagram shows our high-level source file calculating the area of a circle.

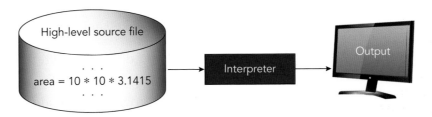

The high-level programming language needs to be interpreted to output a result.

Compiler

A **compiler** translates the entire source code into a machine code file. This file can then be executed.

Key term

A **compiler** is a piece of translation software that converts high-level source code into machine (object) code.

Question

Describe the difference between an interpreter and a compiler.

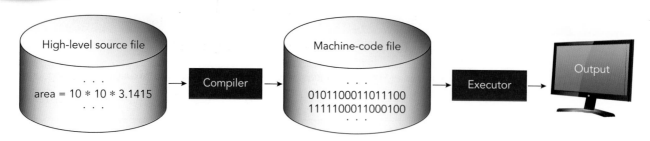

The high-level programming language needs to be translated into a machine code file by a compiler before being executed.

What makes good code?

One answer to what makes good code, of course, is that a program must work and be efficient. The code also needs to be clear so that it can be updated and amended at a later date.

Making code clear can be achieved by blocking similar functions within the code together but also by using:

- comments
- descriptive variable names
- indentation.

Comments/annotation

Good code is well written and well annotated. There are programmers who argue that comments are not necessary if the code is well written, but you will be taking an exam and you need to tell the examiner what your code does and why.

Comment tags remind you and the examiner why you included certain functions. They make later maintenance easier for you.

Have you ever tried to work with someone else's complicated spreadsheet or database? It's not easy. Imagine how difficult it is if you're looking at someone else's programming code.

When you fully document your code with comment tags you are answering (at least) three questions:

- Where is it?
- Why did I do that?
- What does this code do?

No matter how simple, concise and clear your code may end up being, it is impossible for code to be completely self-documenting. Even with very good code it can only tell the viewer *how* the program works; comments can also say *why* it works.

Key point

Good code should be well written and well annotated.

Question

What is a comment?

Question

Describe the main reasons why programmers would wish to annotate or add comments to their code.

Choose good descriptive names for variables

The variable name should be as descriptive as possible.

Do not use generic names for variables. Adding descriptive variable names improves the overall quality of the software. It makes it much easier to modify and read the code.

Here is a golden rule: spend a few minutes thinking about your variable names before you use them in your code.

If you find yourself writing variable names as soon as you need them in your code, without even thinking about their names for a second, you are probably picking poor names for them. Similarly, if you revisit your code and cannot understand what a variable is from its name, it's a bad name.

Indentation

Indenting is adding spaces or tabs in front of 'blocks' of code (such as *if–end–if*) so that it is easier for you and other people to see how the code flows. It shows which parts of the code will run under certain situations.

Why should you indent your code?

There are several benefits to indenting your code, including the following:
- If you have used the same kind of code structure several times (such as one *if–end–if* inside another), it is easy to work out which 'end of block' goes with which 'start of block'.
- Indenting has no effect on how the code runs, and does not alter the size of your finished program.
- It is much easier to notice if a line of code is in the wrong place, for example after an *end if* when it should be before the *end if*.
- Users can immediately ignore chunks of the code that are not relevant to what they are currently doing.
- Users can see at a glance where the end of a code block is rather than having to read each line until they find it.

In Python you are forced to indent parts of the code, but it is good practice to do this in any coded solution.

Is white space more significant in Python source code?

No, not in general. Only the indentation level of your statements is significant (that is, the white space at the very left of your statements). Everywhere else, white space is not significant and can be used as you like, just like in any other language.

Question

Describe the main reasons why it is important to choose descriptive names for variables.

Key point

White space is a useful tool in any coded solution as it helps to separate the blocks of code.

What does the following function return?

```
<code>
list(range(10))
</code>>>>
list(range(10))
```

You can also insert empty lines that contain nothing (or only arbitrary white space) anywhere.

The exact amount of indentation does not matter either; only the relative indentation of nested blocks (relative to each other) is important.

Errors

You now know why you have to produce well-documented, efficient code, all laid out well with good use of white space. You may think all is well but however much you tried to avoid errors, they are inevitable in any program.

Even if you coded your program perfectly, the users of your program will always discover some problem in your application that you never even dreamed was possible.

Although it is impossible to eliminate every error, this section should help you to avoid most coding errors.

Different types of errors in computer programming

As much as we may wish to deny it, human beings are not perfect. We make mistakes. Programmers are not exempt from this (as most are human) and make errors in the programs they create. These errors lead to problems, defects or, as they are most commonly known, bugs. The process of fixing these mistakes, of removing the bugs, is known as debugging.

Key point

If you write 12 or more lines of code expect to find a syntax error, a bad array reference or a misspelled variable. This is quite normal.

There are three types of errors that computer programmers make when writing code. These are:

- syntax errors
- runtime errors
- logic errors.

Syntax errors

Syntax errors, or as they are sometimes known, format errors are a big problem for those who are new to programming. A syntax error occurs when the programmer fails to obey, usually through inexperience, one of the grammar rules of the programming language that he or she happens to be using to write the application. Typically, this might be because of using the wrong case, placing punctuation in positions where it should not exist or failing to insert punctuation where it should be placed within the code.

Some programming languages that are specifically designed to introduce people to programming use a drag-and-drop method of writing code, where the user clicks and drags snippets of code into the place in the program where they are needed. This allows the programmer to concentrate on creating a solution to a programming problem with a robust structure without having the added distraction of satisfying syntax requirements.

Question

See if you can identify the syntax error in the following:

```
counter = 0
While counter < 5
    print "hello"
    counter = counter + 1
```

Runtime errors

Runtime errors happen whenever a program instructs the computer to carry out an operation that it is either not designed to do or reluctant to do. As a consequence of the huge number of situations that can be categorised within this area there is equally a huge number of ways to write programs that cause runtime errors.

Question

What is a runtime error?

In some programs, runtime errors commonly occur when programming statements are written in the wrong order or a programmer writes instructions that the computer is unable to carry out. One of the most common runtime errors is when a program instructs a computer to divide any number by the value zero. This operation produces an infinitely large result, which consequentially is too large for a computer to accommodate. In this situation the computer will return an error message informing the user that it is unable to perform that operation.

Question

Explain the following statement: 'Run-time Error 339 component MCI32.OCX or one of its dependencies is not correctly registered: a file is missing or invalid.'

Logic errors

Out of the three common programming errors, logic errors are typically the most difficult kind to detect and correct. This is usually because there is no obvious indication of the error within the software. The program will run successfully; however, it will not behave in the designed manner. In other words it will simply produce incorrect results.

Question

What is meant by a logical error? Give an example of a logical error in your chosen programming language.

Question

A programmer is developing a new program. Describe the types of errors he or she should check for.

Logic errors are usually a consequence of one of the following:

- Careless programming.
- The programmer did not understand the individual behaviour of each operation that was part of the program.
- The programmer did not understand the manner in which the program was meant to behave.

It is worth noting that logic errors can often remain undetected until an angry user contacts the programmer to say that their program has performed some disastrous operation such as paying all the employees of a company too much in their monthly salaries!

How can logic errors be prevented? Well, the following rules should prevent most of the errors:

- Avoid careless programming.
- Implement a thorough and rigorous testing strategy.
- Programmers should fully understand how a finished program is meant to behave.
- Programmers should have a thorough knowledge of the behaviour of every operation that is written into the program.

Testing for errors before and during the coding stages

It is important to test a system thoroughly in order to ensure that it is robust and not likely to malfunction. However, it should be understood that a program is very unlikely to work perfectly the first time it is executed. Therefore, testing is carried out on the code to try and make it fail and reveal the presence of errors. If software is not tested effectively the consequences could be one or more of the following:

- It could cause a serious accident, for example if the code is part of a program that runs a system on an aircraft or in a nuclear power station.
- It could ruin the reputation of the company that has written the program.

Later we will look at debugging. This is the process of detecting and correcting errors during execution of the program; however, in this section we will look at how errors can be detected prior to running the program.

Dry-run testing

Dry-run testing is usually carried out on the algorithm, which is written in pseudocode or as part of a flowchart. This form of testing is usually done before the program code is written.

The process involves the stepping through of the algorithm one instruction at a time with purposely chosen example test data. A programmer uses a 'trace table' to keep track of the test data, its purpose being to demonstrate what went wrong within an algorithm and to locate the problem. It should be understood that this form of testing is usually done on a small scale as it is quite hard work and very repetitive.

Proving code correctness using unit testing

If a programmer has only to check the correctness of the code within a small program, he or she may just go through the program line by line checking for errors manually. This is tedious enough with a small program and is also open to human error, so you can imagine that with large programs this process of proving code correctness is completely unfeasible. Therefore, professional program developers use software tools called unit tests.

Unit testing is a popular practice that consists of writing additional programs that test individual functions of the main program under development. Unit tests are small pieces of code whose purpose is to prove the correctness of aspects such as methods of software modules.

Unit testing is an important process as it is an automatic tool that can uncover 'regressions'. These are unwanted changes in previously working code, which may have inadvertently been introduced during development.

Like with other software, there are effective and ineffective unit tests. A poor unit test will focus on a situation that is not relevant for the application, while a good quality unit test is one that is written to catch cases such as where someone enters a negative value as a salary figure.

'Code coverage' is a term that is used to describe the percentage of lines of code that are considered by unit tests. It should be realised that there is no relationship between the number of unit tests applied to a program and the potential correctness of the code.

Testing for errors during the execution of code

The process of testing a program for errors during its execution is a cyclic activity called **debugging**. To debug code effectively, two things are needed:

- The ability to test each of the instructions provided by a program.
- The capability to retrieve information back about:
  - the results of those instructions
  - any changes in the program when the tests were carried out
  - the error conditions
  - what the program was doing when the error occurred.

Fortunately, there are software tools that can assist in the debugging process. These tools are called **debuggers** and the source code of a program is run through these in order to detect syntax, runtime and logic errors. The debugger produces a report that highlights and lists error information to the program tester.

There are a number of specific features within debuggers that can assist the program tester in detecting errors, such as:

- breakpoints
- steps
- trace tables
- watchers.

Breakpoints

Breakpoints are breaks that can be inserted manually into code by the tester in order to halt the execution of the program at specific points. This allows the tester to inspect the code at those points. Usually, code on the line where a breakpoint has been inserted will be highlighted in a red or yellow colour. Any number of breakpoints can be inserted into a program, although a situation is reached when there really is no reason to insert any more breakpoints.

Steps

Once the program is paused (say by a breakpoint), the debugger allows the tester to continue the execution of the program one line at a time – effectively stepping through the program. This allows a programmer the capability to see exactly how many variables and objects are affected when a particular line is executed.

Watchers

A watcher is usually in the format of a table and displays the values of specified fields and variables relative to the particular line that the debugger is currently on. Most debug programs have a watch window and a QuickWatch dialogue box. These are places where you can enter variable names and expressions that you want to watch during a debugging session. To add a watch, the tester usually types the name of the variable he or she is interested in within an area of the user interface of the debugging program.

Expressions that require evaluation, such as $x + 1$ or array accesses, can be typed into a watch.

Question

Describe four methods that a programmer can use to test for errors when programming.

Trace tables

A **trace table** is a technique used to test algorithms to see if there are any logic errors in the algorithm being processed.

Within the table, each column contains a variable and each row displays each numerical input into the algorithm and the resultant values of the variables.

Trace tables are particularly popular with people who are learning to program.

Testing

In general, testing is finding out how well something works. For example, you will be tested in your understanding of computing. In this sense testing indicates what level of knowledge or skill you have acquired.

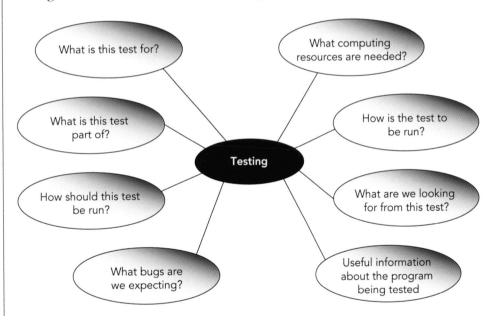

A spider diagram summarising software testing.

Software testing is similar. It is much more than just error detection. Testing software is operating the software under controlled conditions to see how well it works.

You will use testing to ensure that the script you have written actually does what it is supposed to do. It is not possible to write scripts perfectly so that they always do exactly what they are supposed to do the first time. And even if it was possible, a user would find something that does not work on his or her machine.

You will need to test all your scripts in order to locate and fix any errors.

Key point

The best way to debug a program is to use the print command to print out the values of variables at points in the program to see where they go wrong.

Why do we need to carry out a formal test?

The reason we need to test and document coded solutions is to enable us to make objective judgements about how well a software product meets, exceeds or fails to reach a set of criteria that are normally stated in the specification.

In order to test your own products, you must ensure that you have a good, clear specification before you start the design phase of your project.

We test applications when we wish to understand and be confident that a software product will do its job well when it is released to other users. The users are often called clients.

Application testing is important in the development of complex applications as it often indicates the end of the development phase. It is also the process that establishes the criteria that a client will use to decide whether to accept or refuse the project.

What are the purposes of testing?

There are two reasons why we test:

- Testing verifies that the application that has been created and delivered meets the specification criteria that were agreed between the developer and the client.
- Testing manages the risk for both the client and the developer. A testing program identifies whether an application has been produced to the specified requirements of both the client and developer so that the programmer's work can be ended and paid for. The project then shifts into the maintenance part of the software development life cycle.

How do you document your tests?

For most programs it is practically impossible to *prove* that the program is correct on all machines and systems with any input. What you do need to do is prove that your program works as stated in the specification. You do this by producing a testing document saying how you intend to test the program and then showing the results of these tests.

This document is called a test plan and you should provide one with each program. Remember to list only measurable things in your test plan.

When should testing take place?

If a basic software development life cycle is considered, testing is usually carried out between the development period and the application launch or handover to the client. For you, this will be before you pass your finished program to your teacher.

Key term

Application testing usually (but not always) involves executing an application with the purpose of finding errors or bugs within the software.

1. Identifier (test plan ID)	
2. Brief introduction (testing objective)	
3. Test items (modules)	
4. Features to be tested	
5. Features not to be tested	
6. Test approach	Which test type (func/non-func/code)
7. Entry/exit criteria	
8. Suspension and resumption criteria	
9. Test environment	Hardware and software needed
10. Testing tasks	
11. Test deliverables	
12. Roles and responsibilities	List of all major tasks to complete the testing effort
13. Staffing and training needs	
14. Schedule	Test estimation

Software test plan

An example test plan.

Types of testing

There are three types of testing:

- Under normal conditions. The application is tested under normal working conditions and the supplied data that a coded solution uses is within the anticipated range.
- Under extreme conditions. The coded solution is provided with data that is within the operating range but at its limits of performance.
- Error behaviour. An application or program is provided with data that is outside its limits of performance. These particular tests try to break the application and to investigate if things occur when they should or should not.

Let's imagine that you have designed a web-based application. Let's also say that the specification stated that the application should run on all Windows-based PCs. The first thing to test would be if it runs successfully in Internet Explorer, the default Windows web browser. There are many

Key point

There are three types of testing: normal conditions, extreme conditions and error behaviour.

different versions of Internet Explorer and each works slightly differently. So we need to test the application in all of the current versions of the browser software.

Since the specification does not specify the web browser, we now also need to test the application in various versions of Firefox, Google Chrome and any other browser that will run on a Windows PC.

Extreme testing could also explore what happens on a mobile browser or a non-PC browser, for example Safari on a Mac computer.

What this shows you is the importance of a detailed and specific specification. If the specification had said to run on Internet Explorer versions 6 and 7, testing would be much easier and less time consuming.

Now let's look at an example of testing procedures with databases.

Under normal test conditions the database is provided with data that is well within its limits, so, for instance, if a field has the limits of 0 and 50, then in these normal conditions the results received should be well within that range.

If a database is tested under extreme-condition testing then data is provided that is at the limits of a field's range, so if a field with the limits of 0 and 50 is tested under extreme conditions then the results that should be received should be either 0 or +50.

Finally, testing error behaviour involves the field with limits of 0 and 50 being subjected to tests where the returned results should be a negative figure or a figure of 51 or more to understand how the software behaves.

Verification and validation

Software development testing is always carried out along with the procedures of verification and **validation**. Quite often you see these two words being used to mean the same thing but this is wrong as they have very different definitions:

- Verification is the testing of conformance (whether is conforms) and consistency of software against predecided criteria. It could be looked on as asking the question: 'Have we built the product correctly?' This is usually carried out with functional testing, where the testing activities verify the specific actions or functions of software code relative to an expected response.
- When we check that an application has been correctly written against a specification that has been agreed with the client it is called validation.

Key point

Extreme data is data that is at the extreme limit of validity and is often used to check boundary conditions. Invalid data is data used to test a program that should always be rejected because it is out of range.

Key term

Validation is the process of checking data as it is input to ensure that it is reasonable.

Question

Explain the differences between verification and validation.

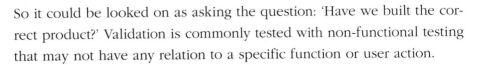

So it could be looked on as asking the question: 'Have we built the correct product?' Validation is commonly tested with non-functional testing that may not have any relation to a specific function or user action.

Non-functional testing

Non-functional testing tends to reflect the quality of the product, particularly the suitability of the application from the point of view of the client. The non-functional testing of applications tends to look at the application as a whole, in other words how well the complete system should carry out its purpose.

Here is a selection of examples of non-functional software tests:

- Load test: the purpose of this test is to investigate software behaviour during increasing system loads. For instance, the quantity of users who use a piece of software at the same time.
- Performance test: to investigate the processing speed and response time for specific scenarios, usually associated with increasing load. For instance, what is the desired performance on the client side of a website? For example, how quickly should web pages appear?
- Robustness test: investigating an application's response to operating mistakes, bugs and so forth.
- Security test: testing for unauthorised access, denial-of-service attacks and so on.
- Stress test: looking at an application's behaviour when it is overloaded.
- Volume test: the investigation of application behaviour relative to the quantity of the data provided. For instance, the processing of large files.

Unit/modular testing

Unit testing, which is also referred to as component testing, is a software development process where the small parts of an application, called units, are individually and independently investigated to see if they work correctly. Unit testing is often automated but it can also be done manually. Unit testing is part of a method of software development that takes a detailed approach to building a product by means of continual testing and revision.

Developers usually create unit tests as they work on code to ensure that the specific function is working as expected. Commonly, one function of the application might have multiple tests to catch certain errors within the code. Unit testing alone cannot verify the functionality of an application, but it is a method to check that the program's building blocks work independently of each other.

Question

Describe the two main types of program testing.

Defining test criteria

When writing a test plan a variety of methods can be used for different testing situations. In each situation, specific criteria need defining and to be agreed between the client and the developer.

Pass/fail criteria

When developers carry out tests on code it is inevitable that some aspects will pass and some will fail. The pass/fail criteria need to be described in clear, unambiguous language and agreed with the client. A process should be defined in advance of the tests to allow the developers to record the problems that occur and also any other issues that they think need correcting.

Pass/fail criteria are sometimes referred to as entry/exit or compliance criteria.

It is common for pass/fail test criteria to be used in the testing of graphical user interfaces (GUIs).

Acceptance criteria

Acceptance testing is a validation test that is carried out to judge whether requirements of a specific criterion or a whole contract have been successfully achieved. The acceptance criteria should be defined clearly and agreed on between the client and the developer. Acceptance criteria test methods should also be defined and agreed.

Within software engineering, acceptance testing may use black box testing on an application before it is delivered or commissioned. Black box testing is regarded as a functional test, which is also referred to as application testing, confidence testing or quality assurance testing.

Alpha tests

Alpha testing is often applied to off-the-shelf applications and is regularly used as a kind of internal acceptance testing procedure before the program is handed over for beta testing. This type of testing can be simulated or quite often operationally tested by potential clients. An outside independent testing house can also test the application.

Beta tests

Beta testing comes after alpha testing and is considered as a type of external user acceptance testing. Beta versions of the application are released to a limited group of users who are unconnected with the

Key terms

Acceptance testing is a validation test that is carried out to judge whether requirements of a specific criterion or a whole contract have been successfully achieved.

Beta testing follows alpha testing and is an acceptance testing by external users.

development team. This particular aspect of testing ensures that when the new software is issued it contains as few faults and bugs as possible.

An example of beta testing could be the testing of an upgrade to an image-manipulation package. First, alpha testing would be done at the software company's site until a specific level of performance had been achieved. After that, and for a limited time, the software house would release a version of the application to a select group of users for beta testing on the users' own equipment.

Test plans and test strategies

People often think that test plans and test strategies are the same documents. This is incorrect as they are dissimilar and have differing purposes.

It is quite a common practice on small projects for companies to include a test strategy within the test plan. For larger projects, however, there is usually one general test strategy document and a range of test plans focusing on each phase of testing.

Test strategies

Test strategies contain an account of the testing approach for a software development life cycle. The purpose of the strategy is to inform project managers and developers about a range of key issues relative to the testing process. These issues include the testing objectives, methods of testing new functionality, details of the total testing time and a description of the requirements for resources for the testing environment.

A typical test strategy document of a software company could include:
- change and configuration management
- communication and status reporting
- defect reporting and tracking
- industry standards to follow
- roles and responsibilities
- scope and objectives
- test automation and tools
- test deliverability
- testing measurements and metrics
- training plan.

Test strategies usually give an account of how risks for the company relative to an application are lessened by carrying out the tests. The strategies also provide a list of the kind of tests that will be performed and what entry/exit criteria (if any) will apply.

Test plans

Test plans are documents that describe the particular approach to each phase or level of testing of an application. The test plan documentation is usually created by the test manager and concentrates on giving an account of what to test, the method of testing, when to test and who will be responsible for conducting each of the tests. The test plan can be viewed as a detailed account of the test workflow, the anticipated results and expectations.

Large test projects occasionally have one master test plan, which is a common document for all the test phases, and each test phase has its own test plan.

Safety and computer use

It is important to use relevant health and safety practices when working with computers. These habits should include regular exercise, correct setting up of workstations, good visibility and suitable lighting.

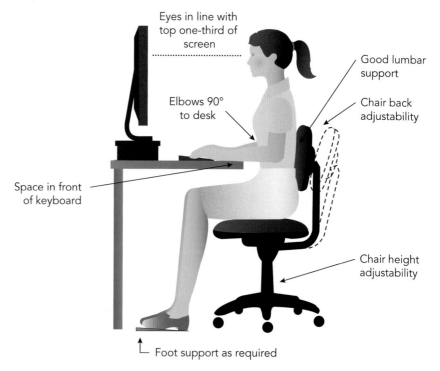

Eyes in line with top one-third of screen

Good lumbar support

Chair back adjustability

Elbows 90° to desk

Space in front of keyboard

Chair height adjustability

Foot support as required

How to set up a workstation for safe use.

Position

Seats should be set so that the forearms are parallel to the floor. Elbows should be level with the keyboard. The computer monitor should be within an arm's length (approximately 50 cm) of the user's face. The top one-third of the monitor should be just below eye level.

Electrical and component safety

Computer scientists are likely to be working within the computer system. Always make sure the electricity is switched off and the plug removed from the socket before touching any hardware. When handling hardware you must keep your fingers on the sides of the circuit board or on some sort of plastic or metal covering to avoid getting the oil from your fingers on any of the delicate electrical circuits imprinted on the board.

If you are changing internal components be gentle with the hardware. You need to make sure that you discharge your body of any static charge that might build up on you before touching internal components of a computer. After you open up your computer it is also best to ground the case of the machine (you can touch something metal before touching the computer). Avoid wool clothing because it can build very large static charges. If a component will not fit, check to see if it is the right slot for that component. If something will not come out, look around the component to check for clips and fasteners.

Settings

When making changes to computer settings, save and memorise the changes so that you can reverse them if necessary.

Moving computer equipment

Never move, slide, bump or pick up the computer when it is running as there is the risk of damaging the hard disk and possibly creating other problems.

Using ICT securely

Why should we use strong passwords, keep anti-virus software and security patches up to date, log out of services when we finish using them, and be careful of the information we send in emails, texts or instant messages? The only time anything is private in computing is when the computer is offline. Never put any private information on the internet. When using online banking make sure the connection is encrypted (https) or you are using an anonymous internet protocol (IP).

It is easy to identify the people around us who could gain physical access to our files, legitimately or not: they include our family, friends and others. But identifying those who can gain access to our information and computers remotely is impossible. This is why using technology safely and securely is so important.

If you practise secure computing, you can at least limit the risk of an unauthorised individual accessing your files and confidential information or installing malicious software on your computer.

Two of the easiest things you can do to keep others from accessing your account or information are to use a strong password and to lock your computer when you walk away from your desk.

Passwords

Choosing a strong password reduces the risk of a security breach of your data, whether it is your personal files, Twitter or Facebook. You should also password protect your computer.

Make passwords complex but memorable. Here are a few suggestions:
- You can replace letters with numbers or special characters.
- You can also use a phrase and turn it into a password.

Using ICT legally and ethically

Much is written about using computers safely, but alongside safety is the law and ethics when using computers, particularly when you start to learn to code.

Legal use

You will have seen warnings against illegally downloading copyrighted material such as films, music, books, software and video games. What you may not realise is that when you begin downloading illegal copies of this type of material, you can also inadvertently begin sharing these files with others. The **IP address** of the computer used to download materials is easy to track, making it possible to identify the responsible individuals.

Getting caught in a legal process is not the only reason to stay away from downloading illegal files. There is also a chance that malicious files have been uploaded to catch out unwary users that contain viruses or trojans which can wreak havoc on your computer.

Question

Describe three main security measures required when using an internet-connected computer.

Key point

Make passwords complicated but memorable.

Key term

The IP (internet protocol) address is a number that identifies a device on a TCP/IP network.

Ethical use

If you access, view or collect confidential material and/or personal information, it is your responsibility to maintain confidentiality. Do not share this information with unauthorised individuals.

Question

What is meant by the terms legal and ethical use in relation to computer software?

4 Constructs

Structure

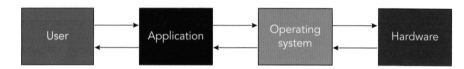

The structure of a computer system.

Everything in computing must have structure. The diagram shows the structure of a system. We have looked at the use of flowcharts to represent the structure of a program in previous chapters. Structure shows the sequence of operations.

Sequence

The concept of one instruction following another in a physical sequence is the underlying structure of any program. Indeed, it could be argued that computer code is simply a sequence of instructions. An instruction is given in the form of a statement. Statements are then executed in sequence until another instruction is reached that changes the sequence. The sequence can contain any number of actions, but no actions can be skipped in the sequence.

A sequence is one of the three basic logic structures in all computer programming. The other two logic structures are selection and loop.

All logic problems in programming can be solved by writing algorithms using these three logic structures. Of course, they can be combined in an infinite number of ways, so no two programmers will write the same code.

The more complex the computing need, the more complex the combination of structures.

Key point

Everything in computing must have structure. The more complex the computing need, the more complex the combination of structures.

Task

Write a simple sequence using your chosen computer language.

Key point

The concept of one instruction following another in a physical sequence is the underlying structure of any program.

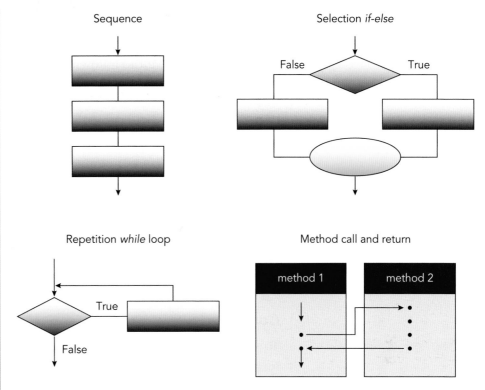

Flowcharts for a sequence, a selection *if-else*, a repetition *while* loop, and a method call and return.

Data types

Understanding data types is essential when writing your own algorithms. We will look at these in more detail in Chapter 5 but in order to understand programming constructs we need to explore them a little here.

First, we know that all data has to be one of a number of different data types. If we look at these in pseudocode the base types are:

INTEGER
REAL
BOOLEAN
CHARACTER

We also have binary operators that in pseudocode model their mathematical counterparts:

equality: =
inequality: =/
less than: <
less than or equal: <=
greater than: >
greater than or equal: >=

Data structures

We also know that all data is structured. If we look at these in pseudocode we have the following:

```
ARRAY: A finite length sequence of same type and
STRING: A string is really just a specialisation of ARRAY
using characters as the data type
```

Each data structure in a program needs what is called an identifier.

Identifiers

Identifiers are the usual sequences of letters and digits, usually starting with a letter. Examples include:

```
myValue
My _ Number counter4
```

Commands

To write a sequence we need a sequential list of commands. These could include:

- variable introduction and assignment command sequences
- conditions
- repetition and iteration subprogram calls.

Repetition and loops

We have looked at how a structure has three essential elements: sequence, selection and loops. In this section we will look at loops in more detail.

The *while* loop is one way of achieving repetition. It is similar to an *if* statement in that it executes the code *if* a stated condition is true.

The difference is that the *while* loop will continue to repeat the code for as long as the condition is true. In other words, instead of executing if something is true, it executes while that thing is true.

If we look at an example in Python, line 4 decides when the loop will be executed. So, 'as long as the count is less than 9' the loop will continue to repeat.

Line 6 increases the count by 1. This happens over and over until the count equals 9 then the repetition stops.

```
count = 0
if count < 9:
    print "Hello, I am an if statement and the count is",
    count
while count < 9:
    print "Hello, I am a while and the count is", count
    count += 1
```

A *while* loop in Ruby looks similar:

```
counter = 1
while counter < 11
    puts counter
    counter = counter + 1
end
```

As you can see, it is easy to identify repetition in code whatever the language used.

Variables

If you look at our loop sequence it has what is called a variable. The type of the variable is inferred from the initialising value, and ours had an identifier called count:

```
SET count TO 0 creates a counter variable, initialised to
zero
```

We can use variables in other ways. We can:

```
SET a TO b creates variable a, initialised to the value
held by variable b
```

Command sequences

The concept of a sequence of commands is one of the major control flow structures in any language. These are also known as *blocks* in many languages. Our counter had a sequence.

In pseudocode, commands are written one line after another in a top to bottom sequence. We can read the command sequence from top to bottom.

Condition

Our counter also had a condition. Conditional commands have the form:

```
IF expression THEN command END IF
IF expression THEN command ELSE command END IF
```

An example of a simple one-armed conditional is:

```
IF a > 3 THEN
SEND "more than three" TO DISPLAY END IF
```

Repetition

Our counter also contained a repetition. The command was repeated while the count was less than 9. Repetition may be specified to take place a fixed number of times in an algorithm, or it may continue until a condition is reached, as it was in our example.

Conditional repetition can place the decision on whether to continue repeating at the start or end of the command sequence to be repeated. These commands are:

```
WHILE expression DO command END WHILE REPEAT command
UNTIL
```

Bounded/fixed repetition

In our repetition, we repeated until a condition was met but this is not the only form a repetition can take. Consider two forms. In the first, code is repeated a specified number of times:

```
REPEAT expression TIMES command END REPEAT
```

or

```
FOR id FROM expr TO expr DO command END FOR
FOR id FROM expr TO expr STEP expr DO command END FOR FOR
EACH id FROM expression DO command END FOR EACH
```

As an example:

```
SET myArray TO [ "The","rain","is","heavy","today" ] SET
sentence TO ""
FOR EACH word FROM myArray DO
SET sentence TO sentence & word & " "
END FOR EACH
```

Selection

The last of our three essential structure elements is selection. In a selection structure, an *if* question is asked called a condition. Depending on the answer, the program takes one of two courses of action, after which the program moves on to the next event.

Let's say the condition ($a < b$) is to be evaluated as true or false (if a is less than b, the condition is true, otherwise false).

An example in C:

```
if(condition){
//do this if the condition is true
}
// this runs after the IF statement. If the statement is
false, the code jumps straight to here.
```

If we use an example (using *if* and *else*) where *else* denotes code that the programmer wants to run only if the condition is false:

```
if(a<b){
// a is less than b
} else {
// a is NOT less than b
}
```

The programmer can set values, and use other selections within selections, which is called **nesting**. You should be able to recognise conditions easily in most coded solutions.

Subprograms

The final thing to look at in this chapter on constructs is subprograms. A subprogram is a program called by another program to perform a particular task or function for the program. When a task needs to be performed many times, you can make it into a separate subprogram.

The complete program is made up of multiple smaller, independent subprograms that work together with the main program.

There are two different types of subprograms: external and internal.

External subprograms

External subprograms are the simplest type of subprogram. They exist as standalone programs that are listed in the program menu, and involve executing one program from inside another program using a simple command, just like a regular program.

Internal subprograms

Internal subprograms are the most complicated type of subprogram. They involve putting the subprograms into the main program itself, so that they can be called by the program whenever needed.

This is not the same thing as pasting the code from the subprogram in place of the subprogram call, like you can do with external subprograms.

Key term

Nesting is adding structures inside other structures.

Key point

In a selection structure an *if* question is called a condition. Depending on the answer, the program takes one of two courses of action, after which the program moves on to the next event.

Task

Write a simple selection using your chosen computer language.

It is coding the main program so that it can take advantage of subprograms, but all the code is self-contained.

User experiences

When an architect designs a shopping centre, not all of the architect's attention is given to the structure of the building. A significant amount of time is also given to how the shoppers will interact with the centre. In particular, the architect must consider visual appeal and the ambiance of the centre's environment. In a similar way, an important part of a software system's design involves the system's interface with the end users. Designing a user interface has become a subject of its own.

5 Data types and structures

> ## Learning outcomes
>
> - Understand the need for and be able to select and use data types.
> - Understand the need for and be able to select and use data structures.
> - Understand the need for and be able to manipulate strings.
> - Understand the need for and be able to use variables and constants.
> - Understand the need for and be able to use global and local variables.

Data types

Primitive data types are predefined types of data, which are supported by the programming language. They are the most common data types and the ones you will be using.

We know that data can be stored in many different forms and that the proper term for these forms is *data types*. In computing, it is these forms that determine what actions, for instance searching, sorting or calculating, can be performed on the data when it is held within a field of a database or a spreadsheet.

Before we get back to coding, let's look at some of the common primitive data types that you will be using.

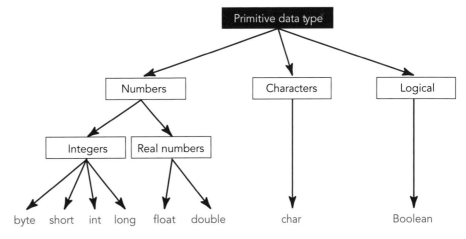

Common primitive data types.

Integer

An **integer** is a whole number (not a fraction), which can be positive, negative or zero. Integer data types deal with whole numbers, not decimal numbers, which use a different data type.

Here are some examples of integers: –9, 3, 5, 8, 98 and 5103.

Here are some examples of numbers that are not integers: –1.33, 1¾, 3.14 and 1500.45.

Some versions of Python can be forced to use a floating point.

```
int (17.0 / 8.0)
    #this will force Python to return an integer rather than
    a float
float (17 / 8 )
    # this will force Python to return a float value
```

Integers are usually subcategorised in accordance with their capability of containing negative values. For example, within C and C++ the data type *unsigned short* can deal with whole numbers from 0 to 65 535, whereas *short* can deal with whole numbers from –32 768 to +32 767.

You will need to research your chosen programming language to see how it deals with integers.

Real

A **real** data type contains numeric data in a decimal form. It is used in situations where more accurate information is required than an integer can provide (remember that an integer is a whole number).

Here are a few examples of where a *real* data type may be used:
- Distance in kilometres (km): 23.62, 3.51222, 109.33.
- Mass in kilograms (kg): 20.666, 32.7.
- Speed in metres per second (m/s): 62.5, 10.2.

But real data types cannot store the actual measurement symbol (km or kg and so on) or the units of measurement, for instance kilometres or metres per second. If you want to use the real data type you must remember to add the measurement symbol separately and print the units after the field displaying the data type.

It is worth noting that in the case of money (currency) the data type can be *real* or *integer*. For small values, it is most likely that decimal places will need to be included and so a real data type is required. However, if the values being considered are large, such as the cost of houses, then it is doubtful that decimal places would be important. In this case only whole numbers would be considered and therefore the integer data type would be used.

You may be asking yourself this: if the *real* data type can hold any number, what is the use of the *integer* data type? Well, there are two reasons why the integer data type would be used:

- Processing speed: the speed it takes a computer to calculate using real numbers is a lot longer than whole numbers held as integer data types.
- Storage: real data types take up more memory than integer data types. Therefore, if decimal points are not required it is better to use integers. One of the common mistakes made by people learning programming is choosing the wrong data types. The use of unsuitable data types can lead to programs behaving unexpectedly, with a great deal of time wasted in trying to understand what is going wrong.

Task

Explore how your chosen programming language deals with real data types.

Char

The final primitive data type we will explore here is char. This is simply a character, for example, the letter 'a'.

Boolean data type

In computer science, the Boolean data type is a data type that has one of two values (usually called true or false; 0 or 1). It represents the truth values of logic and Boolean algebra.

- *AND*. The AND operator ensures that all the statements are met before returning a value.
- *OR*. Many people think the Boolean OR operator is an either/or operator: it is *not*. The OR operator is interpreted as 'at least one statement is required before returning a value'. In Boolean search engines more than one or all can be returned.
- *NOT*. The NOT operator excludes the stated item, so the query will return a value based on whether or not something matches the requirement.
- *XOR*. This means that only one of the statements must be true.

In summary, if we have two statements:
- AND means both must be true
- OR means one or the other or both must be true
- NOT means negation
- XOR means one or the other must be true, but not both.

If we look at this in table form:

OR		
input	input	output
1	1	1
1	0	1
0	1	1
0	0	0

AND		
input	input	output
1	1	1
1	0	0
0	1	0
0	0	0

XOR		
input	input	output
1	1	0
1	0	1
0	1	1
0	0	0

NOT	
input	output
1	0
0	1

Further information on data types

Basic primitive data types may include the following:

- Boolean, logical values of true and false
- character (character, char)
- fixed-point number (fixed) with a variety of precisions and a programmer-selected scale
- floating-point number (float, double, real, double precision)
- integer (integer, int, short, long, byte) with a variety of precisions
- reference (also called a pointer or handle), a small value referring to another object's address in memory, possibly a much larger one.

There are some more sophisticated data types that you will come across and which can be built in. These include the following:

- complex numbers in Fortran, C (C99), Lisp, Python, Perl 6, D
- hash tables in various guises, in Lisp, Perl, Python, Lua, D
- linked lists in Lisp
- rational numbers in Lisp, Perl 6
- tuples in ML, Python.

Basic programming concepts

In computer programming you have to first work out the correct sequence of the commands. This may sound easy but let's look at an example to show how careful you need to be. Your friend's postal address may look like this:

John Smith

22 Holly Road

Hempton

London

You know that this is the order that you should write an address, but this is the exact opposite of the way that the postal system works. Royal Mail needs to know the address in the logical task order. This means the order that you use to deliver post: London first, then the area, then the road and finally the house number.

In some countries, the conventional order follows the logical task order. In Russia, for example, letters are addressed in exactly the opposite order to the UK, with the city first.

For your programming to work correctly, all the commands have to be there *and* they need to be in the correct order.

Key point

Many computer programmers label their files using the date format of year, month and day as this is the logical way to automatically list them. The year is the first piece of data required, the month the next and the day last. This is because there can be 12 files with the same day number in a single year.

Question

Create a set of statements for the following paragraph and put them in a logical processing sequence:

'I get up early and open all my presents on Christmas Day. My dad creeps into my room hoping not to wake me late at night, but I often just pretend to be asleep. It's my mum and dad's fault really as they insist that I go to bed early on Christmas Eve.'

Data structures

We can use sentences to show structures or we can use diagrams.

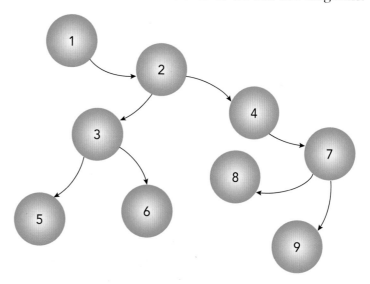

Data structures are a series of sequences.

Computer programming is all about creating a set of instructions to complete a specific task. You do this in your everyday life but you just don't think of it in a programming way. Let's look at an example: you get home from school and want to make yourself a jam sandwich. You know that you will first need to get two slices of bread, butter each piece, spread the jam, and finally put the two together. You cannot put the jam on the bread first or put the slices of bread together before you spread the butter and jam. Everything has a correct sequence.

In this sense, your life is full of sequences and you are always programming sequences in your head. To create any food you have to follow a recipe. A recipe, like a correctly sequenced program, is useful for replicating an action.

But programs are not only useful for reproducing set actions that always follow the same order. Young children create quite complex programming. When they play games such as rock, paper, scissors, they are creating what is called an *if* statement. If you have rock and I have paper, I win. But if you have rock and I have scissors, you win. This simple game has all of the elements of a program: it is a set of sequences and actions performed based on the outcome of what is called a process and repetition (once the game is complete you start again).

In the context of computing, programming means creating a set of instructions, not for a human to make, but for a computer to carry out. These actions are performed in order to accomplish a specific task.

In this section we will explore programming sequences using a programming language that both you, the programmer, and the computer operating system can understand.

The study of data structures is about organising data so that it is suitable for computer processing. This is one of the most important aspects of computer science.

Computer hardware views storage devices such as internal memory and disks as stores of elementary data units, each of which is accessible through its address.

Most data structures can be viewed as simple containers that can be used to store a collection of objects of a given type. The container could be a sentence. The objects (actions within the sentence) are called the elements of the container.

You will have thought about data structures when you first learned about computers. The files and folders you use are part of a simple data structure, in the same way programmers have to think about the data structure in their code. In your friend's address, the city has areas, the areas have roads, roads have houses and your friend is one of the people in a particular house.

Defining data structures

A data structure can be defined as a collection of different data elements that are stored together in a clear, structured form.

In programming, one of the most important design decisions involves which data structure to use. Arrays and linked lists are among the most common data structures, and each is applicable in different situations.

Arrays and linked lists are both designed to store multiple elements, most often of the same type. An array is an ordered arrangement of data elements that are accessed by referencing their location within the array. A linked list is a group of elements, each of which contains a pointer that **concurrently** points to the following element.

Why do we use data structures?

Data structures are used in almost all of today's program or software solutions as they provide a method of managing huge amounts of data efficiently, for example, this could be in a large database or an internet-indexing service. In most programming situations, efficient data structures are the key to designing efficient algorithms. In fact, some formal software design methods and programming languages emphasise data structures, rather than algorithms, because they are regarded as the important organising factor in software design.

What is an array?

Think of computer memory as being like a small or large town, depending on the amount of memory available in the computer. Each byte of memory is a building with its own address called a memory address. The town has people living inside the buildings as bits of data. The small town inside your computer is a very neighbourly place. A program refers to buildings by name rather than by address, and puts Steve's data inside Steve's building. However, you need to come up with hundreds of names for hundreds of buildings. To do this, you can use an array.

An array is a way to reference a series of memory locations (buildings) using the same name. Each memory location is represented by an array element. An array element is similar to one variable except it is identified by an index value, not a name. An index value is a number used to identify an array element.

Key term

Concurrently means happening at the same time as something else.

There are many situations during the writing of code when programmers need to hold related data as a single item and then use an index value to access it, for example, a list of employees' names or makes of car.

One method of doing this would be to assign a variable to each item in the list, such as:

```
name = "Jim"
girl = "Susan"
man = "Bill"
```

Now, although this method does work, what if you wanted to find out what the second name was? The answer is that with this system you have no way of knowing, as there is no positional information contained within the assigned variables. To be able to do this we need what is called a one-dimensional array.

Key point

A one-dimensional array is a list of variables. To create an array, you first must define an array variable of the desired type.

One-dimensional arrays

One-dimensional arrays in Python and PHP are data structures that allow a list of items to be stored with the capability of accessing each item by pointing to its location within the array, for example:

```
carMakers = ["Ford", "Land Rover", "Vauxhall", "Nissan",
"Toyota"]
```

The first line of code defines a variable called *carMakers* as an array, which is storing a number of items. Now, let's say that you wish to access the fifth car make (Toyota); what you do is use a position number, for example:

```
car _ name = carMakers[4]
```

This line of code will return the fifth car make in the array. The process of using a position number is called *indexing* and the position number is called the *index*. The items within the array are called the array *elements*.

The reason why this type of array is referred to as a one-dimensional array is that it only uses a single number to point to the position of array elements.

Question

Explain the term one-dimensional array.

Key point

It is common practice in programming for the first element within an array to be given an index of 0 rather than 1, because 0 is considered by most mathematicians to be a real number between −1 and 1. So, in languages where arrays are positively indexed, zero is the first number (−1 is not possible, the first possible value then is 0).

In the *carMakers* example above the elements would be indexed as follows:

car _ name = carMakers[0]	(would return Ford)
car _ name = carMakers[1]	(would return Land Rover)
car _ name = carMakers[2]	(would return Vauxhall)
car _ name = carMakers[3]	(would return Nissan)
car _ name = carMakers[4]	(would return Toyota)

Table arrays

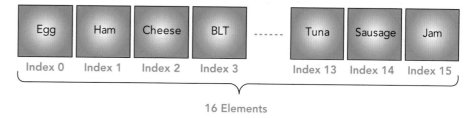

A tableData array showing 16 different types of sandwich.

Sometimes arrays are stored separately. In a table array, just as we explored above, each of the array elements is identified or accessed by an index. An array with 10 elements will have indices from 0 to 9. That means, tableData[0] returns the first element of the tableData array. The correct way to identify an element is to use a pointer. The code *points* to the element.

Two-dimensional arrays

Two-dimensional arrays are a little more complex than the one-dimensional versions but really they are nothing more than an array of arrays. In other words, there is an array in one row and another in the next row.

The best way of understanding a two-dimensional array is to think of it as a way of holding and accessing information within a matrix or grid made up of rows and columns, such as the one here:

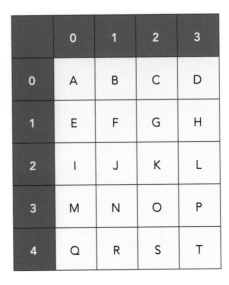

A two-dimensional array.

Let's give this array the name 'letters'. Notice that we have five rows and four columns.

If you wished to define this two-dimensional array as a data structure, in code you would write it as follows:

```
letters[5][4]
```

What we have here is the name of the array – 'letters' – followed by a declaration (in square brackets) of how many arrays there are within the main array, which in this case is five (0, 1, 2, 3, 4) and finally a declaration (again in square brackets) of how many elements there are in each of the sub-arrays – in this case there are four (A, B, C, D or E, F, G, H, for example).

The output from the array looks like this:

Letters [0] [0]	and returns element 'A'
Letters [0] [1]	and returns element 'B'
Letters [0] [2]	and returns element 'C'
Letters [0] [3]	and returns element 'D'
Letters [1] [0]	and returns element 'E'
Letters [1] [1]	and returns element 'F'

We can even use this type of array to define an image. Think about the pixels in a digital photograph.

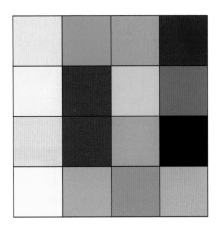

This is how a colour photograph's pixels look when viewed close up.

A digital photograph is simply a two-dimensional array. Conceptually, the pixel values for any image would be represented as a two-dimensional array. The number of columns corresponds to the width of the image (in pixels) and the number of rows corresponds to the height of the image (also in pixels). For example, an image that is 640 pixels wide by 480 pixels high would be stored in memory as a two-dimensional array having 640 columns and 480 rows.

Two-dimensional arrays are used in gaming as well.

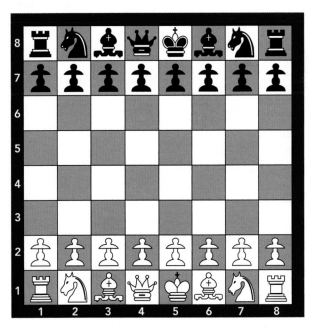

A chess board.

Suppose we want to store information about a chess game. We want to store information about what pieces are in which locations. The most natural way to store it would be to index locations by the row and column. This is done easily with a two-dimensional array. To access the

Question ❓

Explain the difference between one- and two-dimensional arrays.

elements within your two-dimensional array you would need to write a small looping routine.

Task

Identify the pieces in the chess game using a two-dimensional array.

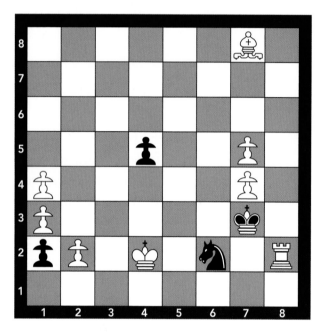

Further on in the chess game.

Representing lists

Data structures: linked lists

A **linked list** is a data structure that makes it easy to rearrange data without having to move data in memory. As an example, imagine a classroom. All of the students are sitting at their desks. The teacher wants to arrange all the students into alphabetical order. The teacher could move everyone around but this would be chaos. And what if the teacher later wanted everyone in height order?

The easiest way is to simply create a list of seat numbers and link it to a list of names.

Linked lists are, by their very nature, one-dimensional. They can appear as singly linked lists or doubly linked lists as shown in the diagrams.

Key term 🔑

A linked list is a data structure that makes it easy to rearrange data without having to move data in memory.

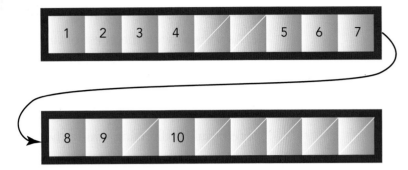

A representation of linked lists.

A *singly* linked list is where the list can be completed in only one direction because the element pointer points to the next element only. The next diagram shows a *doubly* linked list, where each element points both to the next element in the sequence and to the previous element.

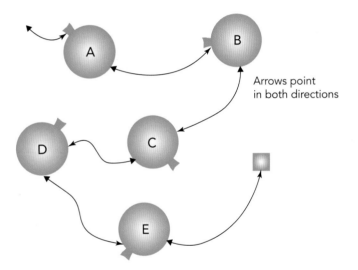

Arrows point in both directions

A representation of a doubly linked list.

Imagine you have a chest of drawers for your clothes. The first drawer has socks, the second T-shirts and so on. In a linked list, the drawers can only be opened in sequence: the first drawer, then the second drawer and so on. With a doubly linked list you can go backwards and forwards but not miss out a drawer in the sequence.

The problem with linked lists is the way that they allocate computer memory. A linked list allocates a space for each element separately in its own block of memory called a linked list element or a node. Just like your drawers, they have a fixed size: your sock drawer is always the same size even if you only have one pair of socks. The list gets its overall structure by using pointers to connect all its nodes together like the links in a chain.

Data structures: binary search trees

As we saw with the chest of drawers example, linked lists require the searcher to examine the entire chest of drawers, one drawer at a time.

An *index* is usually associated with a large, randomly accessed file in a computer system. This, like adding labels to your chest of drawers, speeds retrieval by directing you to the small part of the file containing the desired item. If you wanted to wear only red clothes, you would need to examine each drawer in sequence in a linked list structure.

In computer science, a **binary tree** is a data structure of *nodes* or junctions that is constructed in a hierarchy. Each node is joined to a maximum of two *child nodes* and every binary tree has a *root* from which the first two child nodes are connected. The child nodes are called the left child node and the right child node.

Now, if a node has no children, then these nodes are usually called *leaves*, and mark the end of the tree structure at that point.

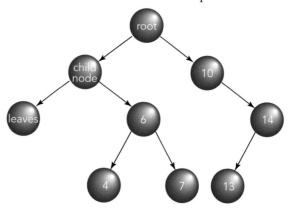

A simple binary tree.

There is a particular kind of binary tree, called the binary search tree (BST). BSTs are very useful for storing data for the purpose of rapid access, storage and deletion.

<div class="sidebar">

Key term

A binary tree is a data structure of nodes or junctions that is constructed in a hierarchy.

Question

Draw a binary tree to show the possible outcomes of tossing a coin eight separate times in terms of heads and tails.

</div>

Task

Design a simple binary search tree to show the party game of pinning the tail on the donkey. Each player is blindfolded in turn and led to the donkey, the player spins round four times, then has to pin the tail on the donkey. The one who has put his or her tail closest to the X is the winner.

Data in a BST are stored in tree nodes and must have a value or key associated with them. These keys are important because they are used to structure the tree so that the value of a left child node is less than that of the parent node and the value of a right child node is greater than that of the parent node. Typical key values include simple integers or strings. The actual data for the key will depend on the program being written and the language used.

B-Trees

A further development from the binary tree is the B-tree. There is no single scheme that is best for all applications but the technique of organising a file and its index into a B-tree has become the most widely used. The B-tree is now the standard organisation for indexes in a database system. The B-tree is the same as the binary tree but it can have more than two child nodes.

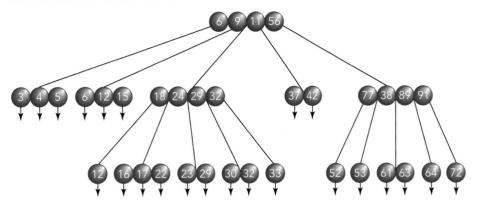

An example of a B-tree.

Why all of this is important to computer scientists

The key (K) in your clothes drawers might be a five-digit number, while the associated information might consist of the type of clothing, colour, size, popularity and year purchased.

We assume that K uniquely identifies a record (called R). We also need to assume that although the key is much shorter than all the associated information it contains, the set of all keys together would be too large to fit into the computer's memory. We need to construct an index to speed up retrieval of the information.

Finally, let's assume that the keys K have a natural alphabetical order, so that we can refer to the *key-sequence order* of a file.

As we buy new clothes we will have to inserte, delete, retrieve and update our records. A set of *basic operations* which support such transactions are:
- add a new record, checking that K is unique
- remove a record K
- retrieve and find data.

Strings

Let's say we want a user to input a **string**. In Python, the input function is used for this purpose:

```
name = input('What is your name?: ')
```

Characters within quotes are called strings. This particular use of a string, for requesting input from the user, is called a prompt.

The input function displays the string on the screen to prompt the user to input his or her name. In most cases strings must be contained all on one line.

A string may contain zero or more characters, including letters, digits, special characters and blanks. A string consisting of only a pair of matching quotes (with nothing in between) is called the empty string, which is different from a string containing only blank characters. Both blank strings and the empty string have their uses.

Variables

The ability to operate on different values each time a program is executed is very useful in coded solutions. This is provided by what is called a **variable**.

A variable can be assigned different values during a program's execution; that's why it is called variable. Wherever a variable appears in a program it is the value associated with the variable that is used, and not the variable's name:

```
num 1 + → 11 + 1 → 12
```

Variables are assigned values by use of the assignment operator =

```
num = 11
```

```
num = num + 1
```

Mathematically, num = num + 1 does not make any sense. In computing it is used to increment the value of a given variable by the value of 1.

Scope

In this section we will look at scope. Scope is an important concept in programming languages. You will not be able to read or write large computer programs without understanding the concept of scope.

The scope of something (function, variable, macro, and so on) in a program is the range of code to which it applies. Let's look at an analogy in everyday life.

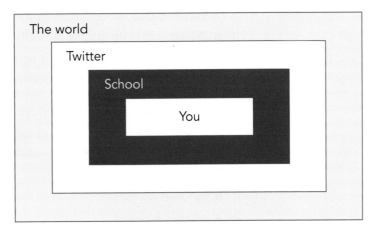

An everyday example of scope.

You have people you know at school or college and have an intranet or chat system that only people in the school can see. You may even have a special language that you use with your friends that no one outside this group would understand. This is a bit like defining a function called *school*, with things that no one outside the school could access or understand. This is the opposite to a global social network such as Twitter, which is not restricted and anyone can see what you write.

So you have a variable that only relates to your school. This would then be called 'local-to-function' scope (local to a particular function; this would mean the variable can only be used inside the function of school). On Twitter, anyone can access what you post: it is global in both real and programming terms (usable from anywhere). The name for this is scope.

Now imagine your program as a virtual world. Parts of it will be restricted to local functions. Other parts are global and can be accessible anywhere.

In some programming languages, special things happen when variables go in and out of scope. Memory may be allocated to hold data, or memory may be freed when variables go out of scope. Scope is also useful for error checking.

The scope of a variable in a program is the lines of code in the program where the variable can be accessed. So the concept of scope applies not only to variable names but also to the names of procedures.

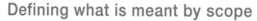

Defining what is meant by scope

When we talk about how variables may be accessed and how procedures may be called, what we are actually talking about is referred to as *scope*. A variable can be declared in a number of ways:

■ When it is only accessible only to a single procedure.

■ When it is accessible to all procedures within a module, and so on up the hierarchy of a project or group of related projects.

There is another term that is used to describe scope and that is *visibility*. You should be aware that the two terms are the same as regards programming and that there are four levels of scope:

■ procedure scope

■ module scope

■ project scope

■ global scope.

Procedure scope

Procedure scope refers to when a variable can be read and modified *only* from within the procedure in which it is declared. Let's take a look at the Visual Basic example below:

```
Sub TestRoutine()
    Dim X As Long
    Dim Y As Long
    X = 1234
    Y = 4321
    Debug.Print "X: " & X, "Y: " & Y
End Sub
```

In the above example, the variables (*X* and *Y*) can only be accessed within the TestRoutine procedure. The variables are created when TestRoutine is called and they are destroyed when TestRoutine ends. It should be understood that these variables cannot be accessed or modified from any other procedure.

Procedure scope has the highest priority of the scope levels, so, in addition to these variables, if you have variables with the same names declared at a *module scope* level (see the next section), the code within the TestRoutine procedure uses the variables declared within this procedure, not the variables with the same name declared at the module level.

Key term

Procedure scope is when a variable can be read and modified only from within the procedure in which it is declared.

Module scope

Module scope refers to when a variable is declared before and outside any procedure within a regular program module. In Visual Basic, if you use the keywords Private or Dim to declare variables, only procedures that are in the same module can read and modify that variable. As a consequence of module-level variables not being part of any specific procedure, they retain their values even after the procedure responsible for altering their values has been destroyed. Let's analyse the following statement:

```
Dim MVar As Long
```

In this statement, the variable MVar can be accessed from any procedure in the same module as the declaration. However, it cannot be read or modified from a procedure that is contained within another module.

You should understand that different modules could declare variables with the same name, for instance both Module A and Module B could have a module-level variable named MVar. Each module-level variable will be read or modified by procedures within the same module.

Now, if both Module A and Module B have a module-level variable named MVar, procedures within Module A will access the variable MVar defined within Module A and procedures within Module B will access the variable MVar defined in Module B. So you can see that variables with the same name in different modules are completely independent of one another, even though they have the same name.

With regard to Visual Basic statements, you can use either Dim or Private to declare a module-level variable that can only be read and modified within that module. To demonstrate this, look at the two statements below – they are basically functionally equivalent:

```
Dim MVar As Long
Private MVar As Long
```

Project scope

This level of variable is declared using the public command keyword and can be read and modified from any procedure contained within any module within the program or *project*.

You should be aware that you cannot declare a *project scope* variable if it has not got global scope (see later). As we saw earlier, to ensure that a variable is accessible from anywhere in the project you must use the public command keyword when you declare the variable. It should be noted, however, that this enables the variable to be accessible to any

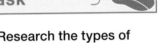

Task

Research the types of scope available in your chosen programming language.

Question

Describe two kinds of scope used in programming.

other project that refers to the project containing the variable. If you just want the variable to be accessible from within the one project, you should implement the option private module statement as the first line of code within the module, ensuring that it is above and outside any variable declaration or procedure.

Additionally, if you do wish to have some project scope variables that can be read and modified from other projects alongside other project variables that cannot be accessed from other projects, it is necessary for you to declare them within unique modules. And to reiterate, the project variables that you don't wish to be accessible to other projects should be declared within a module containing the option private module first-line directive.

Global scope

The final level of variables is called *global scope* variables. These variables have the capability of being accessed from anywhere within the project that contains their declaration as well as from other projects that refer to that initial project.

In order to declare a global scope variable, you use the public keyword within a module that does not contain the option private module directive. To access variables within another project, you simply use the variable's name. However, care should be taken if it is believed that the calling project also contains a variable of the same name. If this is the case then you need to prefix the variable's name with the project name. Let's illustrate this with an example.

If you have a Project A that declares a variable as AnyVarib and Project B refers to Project A, then the code within Project B has the capability to read and modify AnyVarib with either of the following statements:

```
AnyVarib = 1234
Project1. AnyVarib = 1234
```

Now, if both Project A and B contain variables of at least project scope level, you will need to include the project name along with the variable.

For the purpose of clarity, it is always good practice when coding to include the project name when reading or modifying a variable that is declared within another project as it enhances the code's maintainability and makes it significantly more readable.

Scope and procedures

The procedures with the keywords Sub, Function and Property are similar to variables in that they also follow the rules of scope. However, that is where the similarity ends as they differ with regard to their implementation.

As we have considered earlier, any procedure that is declared within a module can be called by another procedure that resides in the same project, unless the procedure utilises the private keyword. Also, if we use the public declaration, it is equivalent to leaving out the scope declaration entirely.

This is all quite complicated, so let's try to simplify it with an example showing how procedures can be called from any other procedure in any other module of the project:

```
Public Sub TheProcedureName()
    Debug.Print "The Procedure Name"
End Sub


Sub TheProcedureName()
    Debug.Print "The Procedure Name"
End Sub
```

In order to write a procedure that can only be accessed from within the module that it is contained in, you must use the private declaration, as shown here:

```
Private Sub TheRoutine()
    Debug.Print "HelloWorld"
End Sub
```

Just as in variables, the public keyword gives the procedure the ability to be accessed by all procedures contained within the project, along with procedures within other projects that refer to the initial procedure.

In order to make the procedure accessible from all parts of the host project, but not from other projects, you can use the option private module directive. As with variables, this ensures that only procedures within the same project can access the initial procedure. So, procedures that you wish to be accessible to other projects should be placed in a module that does not include the option private module directive, but this directive should be included in all other modules.

Python and scope

Let's look at an example of scope in Python 2.7:

```
total = 0; # We set the counter to 0, this is global
variable.
def sum( arg1, arg2 ): # Function definition is here
   total = arg1 + arg2; # Add both the parameters and
   return them."
   # Here total is local variable.
   print "Inside the function local total : ", total
   return total;
# Now you can call sum function
sum( 10, 20 );
print "Outside the function global total : ", total
```

would return:

```
Inside the function local total : 30
Outside the function global total : 0
```

Built-in (Python)
Names preassigned in the built-in names module

Global (module)
Names assigned at the top level of a module file, or
declared global within the file

Enclosing function locals
Names in the local scope of any and all enclosing
functions from inner to outer

Local (function)
Names assigned in any way within a function
and not declared global in that function

A summary of scope in Python.

When a variable is referenced, Python searches for it in the following order:

- in the local scope
- in any enclosing functions' local scopes
- in the global scope
- in the built-in scope.

The first occurrence wins.

Task

Write a short piece of code that includes a scope statement in your chosen programming language.

Task

See if you can work out what the following code will do:

```
function roll () {
  return mt _ rand(1,6);
}
echo roll();
```

Complete the code in your chosen programming language.

6 Input/output

Learning outcomes

- Be able to write code that accepts and responds appropriately to user input.
- Understand the need for and be able to implement validation.
- Be able to write code that outputs information to a screen, and understand and use Cartesian *x/y*-coordinates.
- Be able to design and code a user interface.
- Be able to write code that opens/closes, reads/writes, deletes, inserts and appends from/to a file.

Inputs and user interfaces

Every **interactive device** has to have an input process and output. In computer science we are interested in the interaction between the computer and the human brain. Inputs to humans are via our receptors. We have a very wide range of input receptors: ears, eyes, nerve endings on hands, feet and so on.

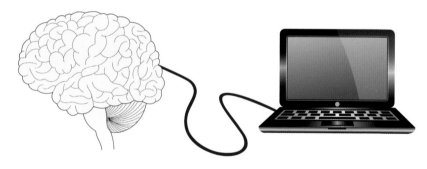

Computer scientists are interested in the human–computer interface.

Computers need input and output devices too. A keyboard and a mouse are input devices. Most screens on desktop computers are output devices. Screens on smartphones and tablet computers are both output and input devices as they have a touchscreen. A camera is an input device and a printer an output device. A games controller can be just an input device, but if it can vibrate it is an output device as well. We will look at many of these devices in more detail in later chapters.

Of course, any input device is only of use if it can link to the user in some way. The user needs to show the computer what it wants it to do.

A **user interface** (UI) is the means by which a user can control a software application or hardware device. A good UI provides a 'friendly' experience, meaning it is easy to use. You will see many manufacturers promoting their products as 'user friendly'. The UI is one of the most

Key terms

An **interactive device** has an input process and an output process.

A **user interface** is the access point and the boundary between the computer and the user.

important parts of any program because it determines how easily you can make the program or device do what you want.

Input can be from physical devices such as the mouse, games controller, keyboard and so on. But it can also be from virtual devices within the software.

Extension task

Identify the inputs, processes and outputs for (a) a smartphone and (b) a modern television.

Nearly all software programs now have a graphical user interface (GUI). This means the program uses graphical controls, accessed via a mouse, touchpad, touchscreen or keyboard.

A typical GUI includes a menu bar, toolbar, windows, buttons and other controls, but new advances in UIs with gesture controls and touchscreens are revolutionising computing in the gaming and the artificial intelligence fields.

A user interacting with a touchscreen on a tablet computer.

Macs and Windows PC **operating systems** have very different user interfaces, but they share many of the same elements, such as a desktop, windows, icons and pop-ups.

Hardware devices also include UIs. A typical television remote has a numeric keypad, volume and channel buttons, mute and power buttons. The remote control is a UI.

While UIs can be designed for use with either hardware or software most can be used for both.

Key term

An operating system is the software that controls all of the computer's hardware. It acts as an interface between the user and the hardware and also between applications and the hardware.

Question

List six input devices.

Output devices

Humans can also output data and information. We can do this with physical pressure and movement using our hands, feet, head and eyes. We can output noise by clapping, talking and singing.

The most popular output devices for a computer used to be the screen, printers and speakers. Today we have a plethora of new output devices from three-dimensional (3D) virtual glasses and heads-up displays to electric paper and voice synthesisers.

Verification

For any device to function correctly, the input needs to be checked prior to any process and output. The name for this checking is verification.

Program verification and validation

The words verification and validation are commonly used in software engineering and usually means two different types of system analysis.

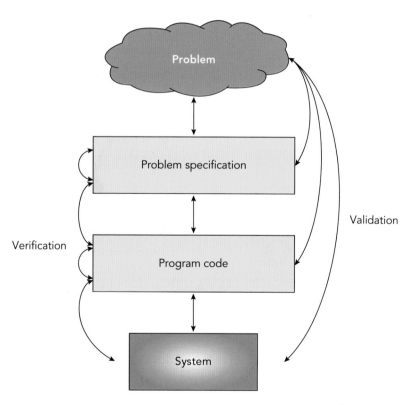

Verification and validation in action.

Program verification

Program verification is about asking whether you are building the system correctly. Verification is concerned with whether the system is well engineered, error free and so on. Verification will help to determine

Question ❓

List six output devices.

whether the software is of high quality, but it will not ensure that the system is useful. Verification therefore includes all the activities associated with producing high-quality software: testing, inspection, design analysis and specification analysis.

Program validation

Program validation is about asking whether you are building the correct system. Validation is therefore concerned with checking that the system will meet the end user's actual needs.

Data verification and validation

Verification and validation of data are two ways to check that the data entered into a computer system is correct.

Data verification

Verification is performed to ensure that the data entered exactly matches the data in the original source. There are two main methods of verification:

- *Double entry*: data is entered twice and then a check is done comparing the two copies.
- *Proofreading data*: this method involves someone checking the data entered against the original document.

Data validation

Data validation is an automatic computer check to ensure that the data entered is sensible and reasonable. It does not check the accuracy of the data.

Let's look at an example. A user of a computer system is thought likely to be aged between 3 and 110 years. The computer can be programmed to accept only numbers between 3 and 110. This is called a range check. However, this does not guarantee that the number entered is correct. For example, a user could be 10 years of age but say that he or she is 16.

Types of data validation

There are a number of validation types that can be used to check that the data being entered is correct. Here are a few of them:

- *Batch totals check*: checks for missing records.
- *Cardinality check*: checks that the record has a valid number of related records.
- *Check digit*: the last one or two digits in any code are used to check that the other digits are correct.

- *Consistency check*: checks fields to ensure data in these fields corresponds, for example, if Title = "Mr", then Gender = "M".
- *Format check*: checks the data is in the specified format.
- *Length check*: checks that the data isn't too long or too short.
- *Lookup table*: looks up acceptable values in a table or an array.
- *Presence check*: checks that some data has been entered into a field.
- *Range check*: checks that a value falls within a specified range.
- *Spell check*: looks up words in a dictionary or an array.

We often use validation in coded solutions, particularly when we have a user input. In Python, for example, we could use:

```
def checkingInput():
    while True:
        try:
            a = input('enter')
            if a == 'y' or 1 <= int(a) <= 10:
                return a
            else:
                print('Invalid input!')
        except ValueError:
            print('Value error! Please try again!')
```

Question

State four types of data validation.

Outputting to a screen using Cartesian coordinates

To position an item on a screen we usually use Cartesian coordinates. Cartesian coordinates can be used to pinpoint where you are on a screen, map or graph.

When using Cartesian coordinates you mark a point by how far along and how far up it is.

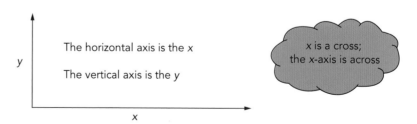

The horizontal axis is the *x*

The vertical axis is the *y*

x is a cross;
the *x*-axis is across

Cartesian or *x*- and *y*-coordinates.
(Tip: remember horizontal then vertical: walk before you climb.)

The *x*-axis is horizontal and the *y*-axis is vertical.

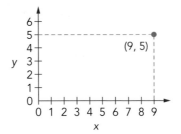

Point (9, 5) is
9 units across (in the x-direction)
5 units up (in the y-direction)

Finding point 9,5 using Cartesian coordinates.

The axes can have negative values by extending the lines to the left and below the 0 and numbering as –1, –2 and so on.

Question

List the values for each of the points in this chart. As an example, point A is (–1,4).

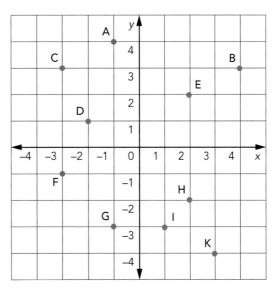

If you need to display three-dimensional objects on the screen you can use Cartesian three-dimensional space (also called *xyz* space). It has a third axis oriented at right angles to the *xy*-plane. This axis is usually called the *z*-axis and passes through the origin of the *xy*-plane.

In programming, points or coordinates are usually indicated by describing them in the following order: an opening parenthesis, the *x*-value, a comma, the *y*-value, another comma, the *z*-value, and a closing parenthesis. An example is $(x, y, z) = (7, –8, –5)$. The origin or centre point is usually, but not always, assigned the value (0,0,0).

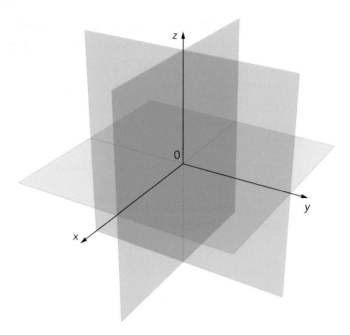

Cartesian three-dimensional space. This is difficult to show in two dimensions.

Writing to and reading from a disk file

So far we have focused on programming logic. Although logic is at the foundation of any program there is one other essential component of programming: reading and writing to a disk file (secondary storage). Disk drives are the main method of supporting secondary storage and providing our programs with **data persistence**. We will explore writing to and reading from a text file.

Writing to a text file

Text files are popular and convenient format that allow programs, created in a range of different languages, to handle external data. Text files offer a common denominator format, which can be understood by both people and computers and provides a method of reading data from and writing data to software applications.

The following sequence highlights the basic steps, within most programs and languages, to work with text files:

- Open the text file.
- Read from or write to the text file.
- Close the file.

When you write information to a text file you are adding data to that file.

A file is usually categorised as either text or binary. A text file is often structured as a sequence of lines, with a line being a sequence of characters. The line is usually terminated by an end-of-line character.

Key term

Data persistence is the ability of programs to save data and return to it and reload that data when the program is run again.

Key point

All programs have to deal with external data. Imagine a program that produces no output and accepts no input. Such a program would be of no use. All programs either accept data from sources outside the coding of the program or they will produce some kind of output. Often they do both.

The most common line terminator is the \n, or the newline character. The backslash character indicates that the next character will be treated as a new line.

A binary file is basically any file that is not a text file. Binary files can only be processed by applications that know about the file's structure.

We will look at the way Python amends text files. First, let us create a new text file and add something to it:

```
file = open("newFile.txt", "w")
file.write("Steve Cushing\n")
file.write("Ian Cushing\n")
file.close()
```

This will create a text file called newFile.txt containing Steve Cushing and my brother Ian Cushing. So what happens if I want to add more data to my existing text file? This time we will do this using a different programming language so that you can see the similarities. If I write:

```
$myFile = "newFile.txt";
    $handle = fopen($myFile, 'w') or die("can't open file");
        $stringData = "Cerri Cushing\n";
            fwrite($handle, $stringData);
        $stringData = "Xian Cushing\n";
    fwrite($handle, $stringData);
fclose($fhandle);
```

all the existing data contained in the file will be wiped clean and I will start with an empty file. This is because the code has used 'w' in the command. In this example we open our existing file newFile.txt and write some new data into it: Cerri Cushing and Xian Cushing.

The program creates a text file when it runs. Within the contents of the directory where the executable program would be located, there would be a text file given a name. If I want to hold the text file in another location I have to define the location.

```
$handle = fopen("c:\\folder\\newFile.txt", 'r');
```

So what do the 'r' and 'w' do? The mode argument, 'r', is optional in many languages and will be assumed if it's omitted. The modes can be:
- 'r' when the file will only be read.
- 'w' for only writing (an existing file with the same name will be erased).
- 'a' opens the file for appending. Any new data written to the file is automatically added to the end.
- 'r+' opens the file for both reading and writing.

Reading from a text file

Before we can read information from a file we have to use a function to open it. In Python we use the open() function.

To open a file for writing use the built-i open() function. open() returns a file object, and is most commonly used with two arguments. The syntax is as follows: file_object = open(filename, mode), where file_object is the variable to put the file object.

We now know that the second argument describes the way in which the file will be used.

If you want to return a string containing all characters in the file, you can use file.read():

```
file = open('newfile.txt', 'r')
print file.read()
```

The output would be:

```
Cerri Cushing
Xian Cushing
```

We can also specify how many characters the string should return, by using file.read(n), where 'n' determines the number of characters. The following reads the first four characters of data and returns it as a string:

```
file = open('newfile.txt', 'r')
print file.read(4)
```

The output will be 'Cerri'.

This is extremely useful as you can add data from the text file to a variable.

If we explore how an algorithm can move through a file a record at a time to read field data into variables it could look like this in pseudocode:

```
open myInFile for Input
open myOutFile for Output
while name not equal to blank

    firstID equals myInFile(1-6)
    firstName equals myInFile (7-20)
    theCost equals myInFile (31-10)
    theCost equals theCost times 1.1
    myOutFile write firstID, firstName, theCost

    close myInFile
    close myOutFile
```

Question

A programmer is developing an online computer game. Describe the types of data he or she might store in a string rather than externally.

The file is opened. A file may be opened for input, output or append. Append would add records to the end of an existing file whereas output would create a new file or overwrite an existing file. The text file characters are then stored into the named variables. If you want to delete or amend text this is one of the simplest ways of doing so, as it works in all programming languages. You simply store the text in a variable then amend the variable and create a new text document.

7 Operators

Learning outcomes

- Understand the purpose of and be able to use arithmetic operators.
- Understand the purpose of and be able to use relational operators.
- Understand the purpose of and be able to use Boolean operators.

Arithmetic operators

Arithmetic operators are operations that can be applied to integers, such as addition, subtraction, division and multiplication. You will already be familiar with these. In addition, we will consider modulus division and integer division.

Addition and subtraction are represented in code by the standard symbols of + (plus) and – (minus). Multiplication and division are usually represented by * (asterisk instead of ×) and / (slash instead of ÷).

Depending on the language, integer division may return a real number or the integer quotient. Some languages have two symbols for division, one that returns a real result and one that returns the integer quotient.

Most languages also have an operator that returns the integer remainder from division. This operator is called the modulus operator, but it may or may not act as the mathematical modulus operator.

Modulus division

Modulus division is simply an algorithm that divides two numbers and returns only the remainder. So, for example:

27/16 = 1, remainder 11
gives 27 mod 16 = 11

You may wonder why this is important, so let's look at an example. Say that I want to know the time. A familiar use of modular arithmetic is in the 12-hour clock, in which the day is divided into two 12-hour periods. Let's say we have currently have the time as 15:00, but you could also say it is 3p.m. This is what happens with modulus division:

15/12 = 1, remainder 3
gives 15 mod 12 = 3

Here are some other examples:

30/3 = 10, remainder 0
gives 30 mod 3 = 0

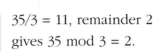

35/3 = 11, remainder 2

gives 35 mod 3 = 2.

Integer division

Integer division is division in which the fractional part (remainder) is discarded. Remember an integer is a number that can be written without a fractional or decimal component.

10/3 = 3 + 1/3

so = 3.

If we look at our previous example where the modulus division returned what was remaining:

27/16 = 1, remainder 11

gives 27 mod 16 = 11

in integer division the answer would be:

27/16 = 1.

Boolean

The **Boolean** data type represents the values of true/false or yes/no. The primitive data type of a Boolean is logical. Boolean logic is a type of mathematical comparison. It is used to evaluate true or false. This may be new to you but it's not difficult to understand.

Consider the following sentence:

If white is a colour and snow is cold then print "ice cream".

Notice how three expressions are being evaluated within this single sentence. We have the two expressions:

If: "white is a colour" AND "snow is cold".

The third is that Boolean logic evaluates each expression to see if it is either true or false:

If (true) and (true) then print "ice cream".

So now we know that Boolean logic is a type of arithmetic **comparison** and that it is usually used in programming to return either a true or false action or a 1 for true and 0 for false.

If the sea is dark and the sky is grey then **print** "rain".

Key terms

Boolean is a value that can only be true or false.

Comparison refers to comparing the values of two items and returning either true or false.

It's important to know that when we have **print** in a piece of code we don't actually mean output it on a sheet of paper. The code never actually prints anything, it just displays it on your screen.

Question

Identify the Boolean expressions in the following:

- When the door is open and it is cold outside I have to wear my coat.
- The central heating switches off when it is higher than 22 °C and switches on when it is less than 18 °C.

Task

Write down the way you get ready for school or college using Boolean. Remember: you need simple if true statements for each thing you do.

Question

Write the following as a Boolean expression:

'When the ground is dry and the sun goes down I water the plants. If the sun is hot and you water the plants it burns their leaves.'

Task

Explore how your chosen programming language deals with Boolean.

Most programming languages could understand this Boolean logic providing we add what are called parentheses:

If (the sea is dark) and (the sky is grey) then print "rain".

Boolean logic evaluates every expression to be either true or false. Therefore, substituting true or false for each of these expressions outputs the following:

```
If (true) and (true) then print "rain".
If (True and True) then print "rain".
```

If either statement was not true, nothing would be printed.

If we look at Python:.

- *x* or *y*: if *x* is false, then *y*, else *x*. The second argument is only evaluated if needed.
- *x* and *y*: if *x* is false, then *x*, else *y*. The second argument is only evaluated if needed.
- Not *x*: if *x* is false, then True, else False. *Not* has a lower priority than non-Boolean operators, so "not a == b" is interpreted as "not (a == b)". "a == not b" is regarded as a syntax error.

Boolean is very important as it is used often in programming, so make sure that you understand it.

In reality, the Boolean data type is hardly ever represented as a single binary digit even though only two values are possible. In fact, many programming languages don't necessarily have an explicit Boolean data type as it usually interprets 0 as false and any other value as true.

Character primitive data types are held in what is called a string, so let's explore what a string is.

Key point

In Windows and Macs, file extensions can be hidden. Your program might not work and you don't know why. You may not see that you have accidentally saved a file as text document and that the software has added '.txt' at the end of your 'page.html' or 'page.php' code, resulting in the saved file being saved as 'page.html.txt'. You will still only see 'page.html' even though it's really 'page.html.txt'. As an added problem if you try to rename the file, it will often not work because it will not overwrite the '.txt' part. You need to change the file type.

String

A string or text data type is capable of holding any alphanumeric character whether it is text, numbers or symbols. It is also capable of storing non-printable characters such as carriage returns as well as punctuation characters and spaces. The data contained within a string data type can either be pure text or consist of a combination of letters, numbers and symbols.

In Python we would define a string by:

```
aString = ("Hello world!")
```

This defines the string aString as Hello World. Anything inside the quotes becomes the value of the string.

```
name = input('State your name?: ')
```

Characters within quotes are called strings. This particular use of a string, for requesting input from the user, is called a prompt. The input function displays the string on the screen and prompts the user for input.

Many programming languages permit the storage of hundreds of characters as a single variable; however, in most situations the algorithm will be storing short string variables consisting of a couple of words.

It is important to note that when you use string data types to store numbers you cannot perform any sort of mathematics on them. The sort of numbers that you would normally store as string data types would be things like telephone numbers where they often start with a zero. If you stored them as an integer the zero would be deleted (remember an integer cannot have a decimal point so 07 is stored as 7). As you never want to perform mathematical calculations on a telephone number the string option is fine.

Key point

Any number that you want to store that begins with a zero must be stored as a string.

Question

Which of the following data would you store as an integer and which would you store as a string?

- Steve
- 2012
- 15
- 10.2
- 007
- marks
- B901LK

Which is the odd one out and what would you store it as?

Date/time

The date/time data type is obviously used to store dates and times. The tricky aspect of this data type is that both dates and times can appear in many different forms. Some countries also have different methods of representing the date, for example:

- 11/06/2014 means 6 November 2014 in the USA
- 11/06/2014 means 11 June 2014 in the UK.

The advantage of using a date/time data type is that you can choose which format you would like your date to be automatically displayed as, for example:

- 23/04/2014
- 2014-04-23
- 23rd April 2014
- 23 April 2014
- April 23, 2014.

Another advantage of using the date/time data type is that the data entered can be automatically validated. Validation makes sure that the data is valid (that is, in the correct format). It doesn't necessarily mean it is accurate, just possibly accurate.

If you entered 30/02/2014 into a field assigned to accept a date data type, for example, it would automatically reject it and return an error message because there is no such date as the 30 February 2014 in the UK format and no 30th month in the US format.

Key point

Valid data is data used in testing that represents normal data that could be expected.

Variables and constants

Now you know about data types, let's turn our attention back to variables and constants. You looked at what these were in your daily life, now it is time to look at them in terms of computer programming.

Variables

Throughout computer programming, variables are data entities whose values can be altered when a program is compiled. As their name implies, their values *vary*.

Key point

Variables are CaSe SenSItiVe.

A *data entity* is a data model that has three parts: a structure, a collection of rules and the operators to be applied to the data.

A compiler is simply a computer program that translates a computer program written in one computer language (called the source language or source code) into an equivalent program written in another computer language (target language or output code).

The compiler produces a machine-language program that can then be run on the computer. For example, Java uses a compiler to translate Java programs into Java bytecode, which is a machine language for the Java virtual machine. Bytecode is similar to machine language and so it runs on the computer much more efficiently. Some computer languages don't use a compiler, but they are much slower as the language needs to be translated as it runs.

When you want the compiler to reserve an area of memory for some values used in your program, you must set a name, also often called an identifier. This will allow you to refer to that area of memory.

The name or identifier can be anything you choose but as with all programming there are clear rules you must follow. In programming the general rules are as follows:

- After the first character of the variable, the name of the variable can include letters, numbers or underscores in any combination.
- The name of a variable can be as short as a single letter but not a single number.
- The name of a variable can start with a letter or an underscore.
- The name of a variable cannot be one of the words that the programming languages have reserved for their own use.

Let's look at some of the restricted words in Java:

abstract	assert	boolean	break	byte
case	catch	char	class	const
continue	default	do	double	else
enum	extends	final	finally	float
for	goto	if	implements	import
instanceof	int	interface	long	native
new	package	private	protected	public
return	short	static	strictfp	super
switch	synchronized	this	throw	throws
transient	try	void	volatile	while

Explain what is meant by the scope of a variable.

Task

Research each of the specific words in your programming language's list of restricted words. What purpose do they each perform?

Question

Why do we use constants in programs?

Task

Research how your chosen programming language defines a group of constants and create a simple program to define an array.

All of these words perform a specific programming task within the Java language so we cannot use them as a name of a variable. You will need to look at a list of restricted words for the language you choose to use.

In Python, the operand to the left of the = operator is the name of the variable, and the operand to the right of the = operator is the value stored in the variable. So with this knowledge let's explore how we can use a variable within program code. We must first define it.

Defining a variable is a similar concept to what occurs in algebra. You will know from mathematics that a value can have a letter or name assigned to it. For example, you could define a starting value of 8 to the variable called Z, therefore in Python we would write:

```
Z = 8
```

So, now at any point within a program where that value requires changing, it can be done by referring to the name of the variable Z, for example:

- Let $Z = 8$.
- Another part of the program then changes it by one of the following procedures, such as:

  $Z = Z + 1$, which adds 1 to the variable called Z, or

  $Z = 5$, which redefines the value called Z, or

  $Z = Y + 1$, which copies the value of another variable called Y, adds 1 and the answer becomes the redefined value of Z.

In computing terms we call this *assigning*, since we *assign* a value to Z.

So, do you understand the idea of variables now? The aim isn't to find out what the actual value of Z is, but to use Z as a storage place for values.

You can even define a group of variables or constants at the same time. As you become better at coding you will find that each language has its own method. Don't be put off by this: the basics of how it all works are the same. If you learn to code with an open mind you will be able to quickly modify your skills to suit different languages. This book has deliberately been written to help you to understand the concepts in such a way that they will become transferable.

Constants are data entities, the values of which cannot change during a program's execution. As their name implies, their values are constant. All data types can be declared as a constant.

Within programming, constants are very useful as they can make the source code simpler to understand. Also, if the value of the constant requires changing at some future point, then it only has to be done at the point where the constant is declared – usually at the beginning of the program.

Classes

A *class* is simply a description of an object. If you were making the object "car", the class would define the parts of a car (wheels, seats, steering wheel, engine and so on) and things you can do with the object (drive, race, park). If we imagine a capsule given to us by a doctor. The capsule is the container. A class is the container.

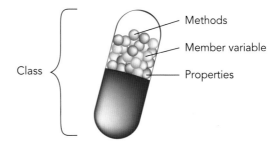

A class describes an object that contains methods, member variables and properties.

Constants and variables can also be used with character or string data types, such as:

```
myName = ("Steve Cushing")
```

Now, at every instance that 'Steve Cushing' needs to appear on the screen, or even on a printout, the variable myName is used.

A common error programmers make is in not using the same capitalisation in a variable. Remember that variables are case sensitive:

- myName
- MYNAME
- Myname

are three *different* variables. If you capitalise your variable in a different way throughout your code the program will not work.

Key term

Constants store values, but as the name implies, those values remain constant throughout the execution of an application.

Key point

Naming your functions and variables clearly is essential as then you won't need to explain how something works or what a particular function does. The name will tell the person reading the code what it does. Anything that can help another programmer or you to better understand your code is worth doing.

Unfortunately, there is no standard method of defining a constant. Each programming language has a different way of carrying out the procedure.

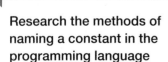

Task

Research the methods of naming a constant in the programming language you will be using.

Should you attempt to change the value of a constant somewhere within the programming code, the debugging tool will usually identify the error and inform you, so use a variable where there will be changes.

Objects

An object is an instance of a class.

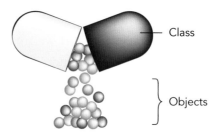

Objects are instances of a class.

In programming, we also use what is called encapsulation. Encapsulation is simply a process of binding variables, properties and methods into a single task or unit. A class is the best example of encapsulation.

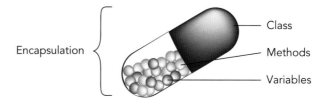

Encapsulation groups variables, properties and methods.

Naming convention for constants

Constants, just as with variables, can be given almost any name. We can define them in PHP using 'define' or $. However, as we can use the variable command $ for a constant, a very popular convention is to use all capital letters for naming constants and lower-case letters for variables:

```
$MYNAME = "Steve Cushing";
$steves _ message = "Good morning from";
print $steves _ message." ". $MYNAME;
```

This code displays 'Good morning from Steve Cushing' on a screen. Notice how the constant $MYNAME is in capitals and the variable $steves_message is in lower case but both have been defined using the $ variable. The reason for using this convention is that it allows constants to be clearly distinguishable from variables within the programming code.

Question

What is meant by a syntax error? Give an example of a syntax error in your chosen programming language.

Key point

Programmers draft their code on paper before typing it into a computer. You should draft the code and check it away from the computer first.

Key point

A logic circuit is simply a circuit made by combining a sequence of Boolean logic gates.

You may be looking at the code and wondering what the semicolons are for. They separate simple statements. Unlike with other languages, in PHP the semicolon before the closing statement and before ?> is not optional: you must put it there. This is why you need to study your chosen code very carefully, as small syntax errors will stop your program from running. You should look at the conventions used in your chosen programming language and learn them. Many programmers have spent ages trying to find why their code does not work, only to discover a simple punctuation error after hours of searching.

A compound statement often uses curly braces to mark a block of code, such as a conditional test or loop. We will look at these later. In these instances in PHP you do not need a semicolon after closing.

Boolean expressions

As we explored earlier, Boolean expressions are expressions that result in a Boolean value, meaning in a value that is either *true* or *false*.

Boolean expressions are made up of the following Boolean operators:

Name	Code	Explanation
AND	&&	True if and only if both sides are true
OR	||	True if either side is true (or both are true)
NOT	!	Changes true to false and false to true

Here are some simple examples in code to make things a little clearer:

Wet AND Cold	$wet && $cold
Rich OR Poor	$rich || $poor
NOT happy	!$happy

You should now recognise the variables $wet, $cold and so on (variables due to the $ sign and the use of lower-case letters) and the use of && (as Boolean AND).

We can actually use brackets (or parentheses) to group complex Boolean expressions together. We explored the use of brackets earlier. They are used to help the programmer and anyone else reading the code, but here they have a different use as the OR Boolean code has been used.

Take a look at these code examples:

```
If (($wet && $cold) || ($poor && $hungry)) {
   Print "I'm sad!";
}
```

The 'print' statement will be executed if the wet AND cold are both true OR if the poor AND hungry are both true.

There are six arithmetic tests that can be used to create Boolean values. These are as follows:

Operator	Explanation
<	Less than
<=	Less than or equal to
==	Equal to
!=	Not equal to
>=	Greater than or equal to
>	Greater than

All the operators in the table have obvious meanings and can be used together with Boolean operators within conditional statements, such as:

```
if ($answer < 0 || $answer > 50) {
   print "The answer has an invalid value.";
}
```

Another example of a conditional statement using Boolean operators could be where you want to test whether a variable *i* lies between 1 and 10, such as:

```
if ($i >0 && $i < 10) {
}
```

Task

Write a simple piece of code that uses at least two Boolean operators in your chosen programming language.

Style within Boolean expressions

There is also a style in Boolean expressions that you should be aware of and use. Let's have a look at a couple of statements, using code, that are written in both a poor and a good style.

Poor style	Good style

`If ( $big_spider == true ) {`
`    Print "Run away!";`
`}`
	`If ( $big_spider ) {`
	`    Print "Run away!";`
	`}`

`If ( $big_spider == false ) {`
`    Print "Relax!";`
`}`
	`If ( !$big_spider ) {`
	`    print "Relax!";`
	`}`

What the table above demonstrates is that it is poor style to compare a condition to true or false as it appears a little silly.

Another aspect of style that should be avoided is the use of double negations, as the following demonstrates:

Poor style	Good style
| ```
If ( !$big_spider ) {
   print "Relax!";
}
else {
   print "Run away!";
}
``` | ```
If ( $big_spider ) {
   Print "Run away!";
}
else {
   print ("relax!");
}
``` |
| ```
If ( !$illegalmove($i,$j) ) {
   move ($i,$j);
}
``` | ```
If ($legalmove($i, $j)) {
   move ($i, $j);
}
``` |

As you can see from these examples, to avoid double negations, Boolean expressions should always be given positive names such as legalMove and gameOver rather than negative versions such as illegalMove and gameNotOver.

Task

1 Write out on paper a short piece of code where the answer is tested to see if it is between 4 and 8 using a Boolean conditioning statement.

2 Write a program to calculate the area of a simple shape such as a rectangle. The length of the sides could be constants and the area a variable.

Extension task

Write a simple program where the user can input the length of the sides of the shape.

8 Subprograms

Learning outcomes

- Understand the benefits of using subprograms and be able to write code that uses user-written and pre-existing subprograms.
- Understand the concept of passing data into and out of subprograms.
- Be able to create subprograms that perform generalisation.

What is a subprogram?

A **subprogram** is a computer program contained within another program. Subprograms operate semi-independently of main programs.

There are two basic forms of subprograms:
- named code that does a particular task
- code that does a task but also returns a value.

The basic idea of a subprogram is to group a collection of statements into a named piece of code that can be invoked by simply calling that name.

In effect we can give a section of code a name and use that name as a statement in another part of the program. When the name is reached in the code, the processing in the other part of the program stops while the named code is executed. When the named code finishes executing, processing resumes with the statement just below the named code. The place where the named code appears is called the calling unit.

The two types of subprograms have many names.
- Ada calls them procedures and functions.
- C++ calls the first a void function and the second a value-returning function.
- FORTRAN calls them subroutines and functions.
- Java calls both of them methods.

Whatever the subprograms are called in your chosen language, they are powerful tools for abstraction. By identifying a named subprogram you will be able to identify what is being done.

Many subprograms are part of a library that comes with a computer programming language. For example, mathematical problems often need to calculate trigonometric functions. The *import this* function in a programming system imports new predefined functions.

Using subprograms

Subprograms are one of the most important concepts in any programming language design. Two fundamental abstraction facilities can be included in programming language: process abstraction and data abstraction.

Subprograms usually have the following characteristics:
- Each subprogram has a single entry point.
- There is only one subprogram execution at any given time.

There are two ways that a subprogram can gain access to the data that is to be processed and these are through variables or through parameter passing. Parameter passing is more flexible than through variables.

Subprograms call statements must include the name of the subprogram and a list of parameters to be bound to the formal parameters of the subprogram. These parameters are called actual parameters.

Procedures and functions in subprograms

Procedures are collections of statements that define what happens to the parameters. Let's imagine that you are washing a cup. Your process of washing a cup could be:
- Soak the cup into soapy water.
- Cover every part of the cup with soap.
- Rinse the cup with clean water to remove the soap.
- Dry the cup.

So, every time you need to wash a cup, you do the same procedure: soak, soap, rinse, dry. You will use the same sequence, repeated over and over again each time you wash a cup. This is a procedure. When you call a procedure in programming it will do the jobs that the procedure is programmed to do. By replacing instructions with one single procedure statement, if makes code easier to read and debug.

Functions are structurally the same as procedures but are based on on mathematical functions. Functions are called by their names in expressions, along with the required actual parameters.

A function is just like a procedure except that it returns a value. For example, somebody may ask you to count the number of cars in a car park. You would go to the car park, count, and then report the number of cars to the person who first asked you. That is a function. A function simply returns another value back into the program, such as complicated calculation results, the position of the mouse cursor or the number of cars that entered the car park.

Functions can report almost anything: numbers, strings, characters, anything. You can even use functions to replace procedures completely. This is the case in some languages where there are no special implementations of procedures.

Return values in subprograms

We now know that functions return values based on mathematical functions. These are called return values. The problem is that return values have what is called scope.

We looked at scope in Chapter 5 but to understand this concept better, visualise a stack of papers on a table. Every time you call a procedure or a function, it will be placed at the top of the stack. When the procedure or function finishes, it is removed. Now, when a procedure or function is gone, everything declared by it disappears as well. This means that if you had declared a variable in a procedure, you cannot use that variable after the procedure finishes, as it no longer exists.

Variables, however, are accessible to those procedures placed above them.

Abstraction and generalisation

Abstraction and generalisation are frequently used together. Abstracts are often generalised.

When you use a name as a parameter it binds the parameter to an argument. The importance of abstraction is its ability to hide irrelevant details and use names to reference objects.

Programming languages provide abstraction through procedures, functions and modules, which permit the programmer to distinguish between what a program does and how it is implemented.

The user of any program only cares about what the program does, not how it happens. In contrast, the coder of the program is much more interested in how the end result can be achieved. The name for this is abstraction. Abstraction is therefore essential in the development of any computer program. It places the emphasis on what an object does rather than how it works.

While abstraction reduces complexity by hiding irrelevant detail, generalisation reduces complexity by replacing multiple tasks that perform similar functions with a single construct. Programming languages provide generalisation through variables and parameters. Generalisation places the emphasis on the similarities between objects and actions.

Functions

The concept of a function is essential in mathematics. Functions are often used in computer languages to implement mathematical functions. The function computes one or more results, which are determined by the parameters passed to it. When the subprogram is called, the calling unit lists the subprogram name followed by a list of identifiers in parentheses.

There are two types of functions:
- built-in functions
- programmer-defined functions.

Functions serve two primary development roles:
- Functions reduce the amount of code needed, as they are the simplest way to package logic for use in more than one place and at more than one time. Functions allow a programmer to group and generalise code to be used many times later. They allow us to code an operation in a single place and use it in many places.
- Functions also provide a tool for splitting systems into pieces that have well-defined roles.

Functions are about how procedures do something rather than what they are doing.

A function in Python is first defined by a *def* statement. Unlike functions in compiled languages such as C, *def* in Python is an executable statement. The function does not exist until Python reaches and runs the *def*. Sometimes in Python it is useful to nest *def* statements inside *if* statements, *while* loops and other *defs*.

The syntax for Python looks like this:

```
def function-name(Parameter):
    statements, that is the function body
```

The parameter can consist of one or more parameters. Parameters in functions are called arguments.

The function body always consists of indented statements. It gets executed every time the function is called.

Parameters can be mandatory or optional depending on the function. The optional parameters (zero or more) must follow any mandatory parameters.

Question

What are the two main roles of a function?

A return statement ends the execution of the function call and 'returns' the result, that is the value of the expression following the return keyword to the caller. If the return statement is without an expression, the special value *none* is returned.

By default, all names assigned in a function are local to that function and exist only while the function runs. To assign a name in the enclosing module, functions need to list it in a global statement. Names are always looked up in the scope where the variable is stored.

Optional parameters

Functions can sometimes have optional parameters. In effect these are default parameters. Default parameters are still parameters, but they don't have to be given as they are predefined in the programming language used. In this case, the default values are used.

The following script greets a person. If no name is given, it will greet everybody:

```
def Hello(name="everybody"):
    """ Greets a person """
    print("Hello " + name + "!")
Hello("Steve")
Hello()
```

The output looks like this:

```
Hello Peter!
Hello everybody!
```

For this small programming task, this function is of no real value, but functions can be very useful when writing code.

Key point

Parameters in functions are called arguments.

Topic 3
DATA

9 Binary

Learning outcomes

- Understand that computers use binary to represent data and instructions.
- Understand how computers represent and manipulate numbers.
- Be able to convert between binary and denary whole numbers (0–255) and the other way around.
- Be able to perform binary arithmetic and understand the concept of overflow.
- Understand why hexadecimal notation is used and be able to convert between hexadecimal and binary and the other way around.

Machine language

Although you will be learning a programming language, computers only understand machine languages. While easily understood by computers, machine languages are almost impossible for humans to use because they consist entirely of numbers.

The computer language you learn will use almost the same instructions as a machine language but the instructions will have names instead of being just numbers.

Humans also use what are called denary (or decimal) numbers. Don't worry about the name, it just means that our numbers have a base of 10. Many people believe that we have a base-10 system because we originally learned to count using our fingers. Humans use the numerals 0, 1, 2, 3, 4, 5, 6, 7, 8 and 9.

You need to have some familiarity with the denary system before we go on to explore binary. To represent the positive integer of 125 as a decimal number we could write:

$$125_{10*} = 1 * 100 + 2 * 10 + 5 * 1 = 1 * 10^2 + 2 * 10^1 + 5 * 10^0$$

The subscript 10* denotes the number as a base-10 (decimal) number. The right-most digit is multiplied by 10^0, the next digit to the left is multiplied by 10^1, and so on. Each digit to the left has a multiplier that is 10 times the previous digit.

You should understand basic multiplication using a base of 10:

- To multiply a number by 10, you can simply shift the decimal point to the right by one digit, and insert a zero to the right (if necessary).
- To divide a number by 10, simply shift the number to the right by one digit (moving the decimal place one place to the left).

- To see how many digits a number needs, you can simply take the logarithm (base 10) of the absolute value of the number, and add 1 to it. The integer part of the result is the number of digits. For instance, $\log_{10}(33) + 1 = 2.5$. The integer part of that is 2, so two digits are needed.
- Negative numbers are handled easily by simply putting a minus sign (–) in front of the number.

Even though computers are based on a binary system, they have to convert the numbers into the denary system so that we can understand them.

As an example, 'Hello World' in binary is:

```
0100100001100101011011000110110001101111001000000101011101101110
1110010011011000110010
```

or in another language, one that the computer can understand, it is:

c7	3c	2a	3c	2a	2b	2a	5c	3c	28	5c	2a	2b	2a	5c	3c
28	5c	2a	2b	2a	5c	3c	28	5c	2a	2b	2a	5c	3c	28	5c
2a	2b	2a	5c	3c	28	5c	2a	2b	2a	5c	3c	28	5c	2a	2b
2a	5c	3c	28	5c	2a	2b	2a	5c	3c	28	5c	2a	2b	2a	5c
3c	28	5c	2a	2b	2a	5c	3c	28	5c	2a	2b	2a	5c	3c	28
5c	2a	2b	2a	5c	3c	28	5c	2a	2b	2a	5c	3c	28	5c	2a
2b	2a	00	00	01	00	00	00	00	00	00	00	00	00	00	00
00	00	00	00	00	00	00	00	00	00	00	00	00	00	00	00
00	00	00	00	00	00	00	00	00	00	00	00	00	00	00	00
00	00	00	00	00	00	00	00	00	00	00	00	00	00	00	00
00	00	00	00	00	00	00	00	00	00	00	00	00	00	00	00
00	00	00	00	00	00	00	00	00	00	00	00	00	00	00	00
00	00	00	00	00	00	00	64	48	65	6c	6c	6f	2c	20	57
6f	72	6c	64	21	00	00	00	00	00	00	00	00	00	00	00
00	00	00	00	00	00	00	00	00	00	00	00	00	00	00	00
00	00	00	00	00	00	00	00	00	00	00	00	00	00	00	00

Every central processing unit (CPU, the 'brains' in the computer) has its unique language (called a machine language). Programs must be rewritten or compiled to work on different types of computers. Let's explore machine language in a little more detail.

Binary

Have you ever wondered why switches have a 1 for on and a 0 for off? It is based on binary computer code. Everything a computer does is based on ones and zeros.

An on/off switch. Why not just use 'on' and 'off' instead?

Question

What is a program written using binary codes called?

Imagine the computer is made up of switches, and each switch controls a light that can be either on or off: one or zero.

Each sequence of on and off lights could represent a different number. To explain the concept we will imagine that we have two lights, each with its own switch. They could be:

■ both off
■ first off, second on
■ first on, second off
■ both on.

Binary code takes each of these combinations and gives it a number, like this:

■ both off = 0
■ first off, second on = 1
■ first on, second off = 2
■ both on = 3.

Perhaps you are thinking that it would take rather a lot of switches and lights to make a computer work like this, but if we had six lights, and they were like this:

on   on   off   on   off   off

and rather than giving a light just one score, we gave different lights in the sequence different scores: the first light 32, the second 16, then 8, 4, 2, 1, the point values of those six bulbs would be:

32 + 16 + 0 + 4 + 0 + 0   (remember – we only give points if they're turned on!)

And that adds up to 52. So we would say the sequence of lights is worth 52. But we would write it as: 110100 (that is on, on, off, on, off, off). This is how computers work and we call it binary code.

Binary representation of positive integers

Binary representations of positive integers can be understood in the same way as their decimal counterparts. For example:

$86_{10} = 1 * 64 + 0 * 32 + 1 * 16 + 0 * 8 + 1 * 4 + 1 * 2 + 0 * 1$

or

$86_{10} = 1 * 26 + 0 * 25 + 1 * 24 + 0 * 23 + 1 * 22 + 1 * 21 + 0 * 20$

or

$86_{10} = 1010110_2$

The subscript 2 denotes a binary number.

Each digit in a binary number is called a bit. So if we want to represent more than four things we need more than two bits.

This table shows numbers represented by one through to five bits.

1 Bit	2 Bits	3 Bits	4 Bits	5 Bits
0	00	000	0000	00000
1	01	001	0001	00001
	10	010	0010	00010
	11	011	0011	00011
		100	0100	00100
		101	0101	00101
		110	0110	00110
		111	0111	00111
			1000	01000
			1001	01001
			1010	01010
			1011	01011
			1100	01100
			1101	01101
			1110	01110
			1111	01111
				10000
				10001
				10010
				10011
				10100
				10101
				10110
				10111
				11000
				11001
				11010
				11011
				11100
				11101
				11110
				11111

The number 1010110 is therefore represented by 7 bits.

Any number can be broken down this way, by finding all of the powers of 2 that add up to the number in question (in this case 2_6, 2_4, 2_2 and 2_1). This is not dissimilar to what we did with the numbers earlier with a base of 10.

As before, we have some simple rules:

- To multiply a number by two, you can simply shift digits to the left by one digit, and fill in the right-most digit with a 0. To divide a number by 2, simply shift the number to the right by one digit.
- To see how many digits a number needs, you can simply take the logarithm (base 2) of the number, and add 1 to it. The integer part of the result is the number of digits. For instance, log 2(86) + 1 = 7.426. The integer part of that is 7, so seven binary digits are needed.

It is quite difficult to convert back from binary as a decimal digit corresponds to log 2(10) = 3.322 bits and a byte is 2.408 decimal digits.

Computers can also use a more computer-friendly system called hexadecimal numbers.

Hexadecimal

It is often more convenient to handle groups of bits rather than individual bits. The most common grouping is eight bits, which forms a byte. A single byte can represent 256 (2^8) numbers.

Memory capacity is referred to in bytes. Two bytes is called a word, or short word.

A two-byte word is also the size that is usually used to represent integers in programming languages. A long word is usually twice as long as a word. A less common unit is the nibble, which is four bits or half of a byte.

It is difficult for humans to write, read and remember individual bits, as it takes a large number of them to represent even a small number. A number of different ways have been developed to make the handling of binary data easier. The most common is the hexadecimal system.

In hexadecimal notation, four bits (a nibble) are represented by a single digit. There is obviously a problem with this since four bits gives 16 possible combinations, and there are only 10 unique decimal digits, 0–9. This is solved by using the first six letters of the alphabet (A–F) as numbers. This gives us 16 hexadecimal numbers.

Hexadecimal numbers look exactly the same as the decimal numbers up to 9, but then there are the letters (A–F) in place of the denary numbers 10–15.

A single hexadecimal digit can show 16 different values instead of the normal 10 like this:

Decimal:	0	1	2	3	4	5	6	7	8	9	10	11	12	13	14	15
Hexadecimal:	0	1	2	3	4	5	6	7	8	9	A	B	C	D	E	F

There are some significant advantages to using the hexadecimal notation for electronic representations of numbers. Using hexadecimal makes it very easy to convert back and forth from binary because each hexadecimal digit corresponds to exactly four bits ($\log_2(16) = 4$) and each byte is two hexadecimal digits. In contrast, a decimal digit corresponds to $\log_2(10) = 3.322$ bits and a byte is 2.408 decimal digits. Clearly, hexadecimal is better suited to the task of representing binary numbers than is decimal.

We always work backwards when converting hexadecimal numbers. For example, if we have a hexadecimal number of 1128 this is calculated as follows:

- The last number is 8. It represents 8×16^0, which equals 8.
- The next number is 2. This represents $2 \times (16^1) = 32$.
- The next number is 1. This will be $1 \times (16^2) = 256$.
- And finally $1 \times (16^3) = 4096$.
- If we add the totals together, 1128 in hexadecimal = 4392 in denary.

You may also want to remember some of the powers of 16:

Powers of 16	Denary result
16^0	1
$16^1 = 16$	16
$16^2 = 16 \times 16$	256
$16^3 = 16 \times 16 \times 16$	4 096
$16^4 = 16 \times 16 \times 16 \times 16$	65 536

You may be asking about the letters. They work the same way, so FA8 working backwards would be:

- $8 \times 1 = 8$.
- $10 \times 16 = 160$ (remember A = 10 and this has to be multiplied by 16^1).
- $15 \times 256 = 3840$ (remember F = 15 and this has to be multiplied by 16^2).
- The total in denary would be 4008.

You now know a little bit about machine language.

Key point

Any number to the power of 0 equals 1. We write powers in computing using ^ so 16 to the power of 3 is written as 16^3.

Questions

1. Write the binary code for the denary number 67. Use seven binary digits.
2. Give one reason why we use binary to represent data in computers.
3. Convert 2000 from decimal to hexadecimal.
4. Convert 3C from hexadecimal to decimal.
5. Convert 1010 0111 1011 from binary to hexadecimal.
6. Convert 7D0 from hexadecimal to binary.
7. If you shift a hexadecimal number to the left by one digit, how many times larger is the resulting number?
8. State the denary representation of the hexadecimal number D48.

Signed and unsigned integers

In mathematics, representing negative numbers is easy: we just add a minus sign. So far we have only looked at unsigned integers. Unsigned integers will not have any plus or minus sign, which means they can only have positive values. We don't always need variables to take negative values, for example: *int age*; age will not be negative. Moreover, we can double the range and store large numbers by using unsigned integers.

A signed integer is one with either a plus or minus sign in front. That means it can be either positive or negative. This is important in computing because the numbers are stored (usually) as a fixed number of binary digits.

One bit is used to indicate the sign for a signed integer. Two common methods are used for this:
- sign magnitude
- two's complement.

Although sign magnitude or two's complement can be used for both positive and negative numbers, sign magnitude has a number of problems and so two's complement is usually recommended to represent signed integers.

Sign magnitude

Sign magnitude uses the most significant bit as the sign bit. The rest of the bits represent the number in the 'binary' format. It is a bit like the number line used in mathematics.

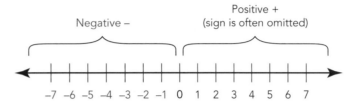

The number line as used in maths.

Performing addition and subtraction with signed integer numbers is easy; you just move a certain number of units in one direction or another. To add two numbers you find the first number on the scale and move in the direction of the sign of the second as many units as specified. Subtraction is the same, moving along the number line as indicated by the sign and the operation.

Look at the binary representation in this table:

Binary	Hex	Decimal
0111	7	+7
0110	6	+6
0101	5	+5
0100	4	+4
0011	3	+3
0010	2	+2
0001	1	+1
0000	0	+0

Binary	Hex	Decimal
1000	8	−0
1001	9	−1
1010	A	−2
1011	B	−3
1100	C	−4
1101	D	−5
1110	E	−6
1111	F	−7

Two's complement

Two's complement is the method computers use to represent signed numbers. The most significant bit is the sign bit:

- 0 = positive value
- 1 = negative value.

The negative representation of a number is created as follows:

- Start with the positive number.
- Flip the bits (change '0' to '1' and '1' to '0').
- Add the value 1. Because of this, a 16-bit signed integer only has 15 bits for data whereas a 16-bit unsigned integer has all 16 bits available.

Addition and subtraction are accomplished in the same way as in denary arithmetic:

−127	10000001
+1	00000001
−126	10000010

There are two advantages of the two's complement method:
- one value for zero
- conversion from positive to negative and from negative to positive numbers is easy and consistent.

Unsigned integers can have a value twice as high as signed integers because one bit is used for the sign. But unsigned integers can only have positive values. You may be asking why this is of any importance.

On older, 16-bit computers this was important, as it translated into a difference between a maximum value of 32 000 on a signed integer or 65 000 on an unsigned integer. On 32-bit computers it is far less significant since we get two billion or four billion, and on 64-bit computers it becomes of academic interest only.

Python has large integers which effectively are unlimited in size, so it does not matter if the integer is signed or not.

Overflow

One problem that can occur with signed binary numbers is that of **overflow**. This is where the answer to an addition or subtraction problem exceeds the magnitude which can be represented with the allotted number of bits. Remember that the place of the sign bit is fixed from the beginning of the problem.

Where a positive number is added to a negative number there will *never* be an overflow error. The reason for this is apparent when the nature of overflow is considered. Overflow occurs when the magnitude of a number exceeds the range allowed by the size of the bit field. The sum of two identically signed numbers could exceed the range of the bit field of those two numbers, and so in this case overflow is a possibility.

However, if a positive number is added to a negative number, the sum will always be closer to zero than either of the two added numbers. Therefore, its magnitude *must* be less than the magnitude of either original number, and so overflow is impossible.

Key term

When a number becomes too large to fit into the number of bits allocated it is said to overflow and some bits are 'lost', leaving an incorrect value.

10 Data representation

Learning outcomes

- Understand how computers encode characters.
- Understand how bitmap images are represented in binary.
- Understand how analogue data is represented in binary.
- Understand the limitations of binary representation of data and how bit length constrains the range of values that can be represented.

Character sets

Text is represented by character sets. A character set is simply a list of characters and the codes used to represent each character. By agreeing to use a particular character set, computer manufacturers have made the processing of text data easier.

We will explore two character sets: ASCII and Unicode.

Representing text using ASCII

For text we use the ASCII standard, which associates a 7-bit binary number with each of 128 distinct characters.

	000	001	010	011	100	101	110	111
0000	NULL	DLE		0	@	P	`	p
0001	SOH	DC1	!	1	A	Q	a	q
0010	STX	DC2	"	2	B	R	b	r
0011	ETX	DC3	#	3	C	S	c	s
0100	EDT	DC4	$	4	D	T	d	t
0101	ENQ	NAK	%	5	E	U	e	u
0110	ACK	SYN	&	6	F	V	f	v
0111	BEL	ETB	'	7	G	W	g	w
1000	BS	CAN	(	8	H	X	h	x
1001	HT	EM	)	9	I	Y	i	y
1010	LF	SUB	*	:	J	Z	j	z
1011	VT	ESC	+	;	K	[	k	{
1100	FF	FS	,	<	L	\	l		
1101	CR	GS	-	=	M	]	m	}
1110	SO	RS	.	>	N	^	n	~
1111	SI	US	/	?	O	_	o	DEL

ASCII stands for American Standard Code for Information Interchange. As we have seen, computers can only understand numbers, so an ASCII code is the numerical representation of characters such as from a to z, @ or even an action of some sort.

Representing text using Unicode

The extended version of the ASCII character set provides 256 characters, which is enough for English but not enough for international use. This limitation gave rise to the Unicode character set, which has a much stronger international influence.

The Unicode character set uses 16 bits per character and can represent 2^{16} (65 536) characters. Compare that to the 256 characters represented in the extended ASCII set.

Here are just a few of the characters supported. The first 256 characters are the same as ASCII.

Code (Hex)	Character	Source
0041	A	English (Latin)
042F	Я	Russian (Cyrillic)
262F	☯	Symbols
03A3	Σ	Greek
211E	ℝ	Letterlike symbols
21CC	⇌	Arrows
28FF	⠿	Braille
2EDD	⻝	Chinese/Japanese/Korean (Common)

Data standards

To help programmers, each data system is controlled by a set of data standards.

Type of data	Standards include
Images	JPG, GIF, TIF, BMP, PNG
Sound	WAV, MP3, AU
Moving images	QuickTime, MPEG-2, MPEG-4
Alphanumeric	ASCII, Unicode
Outline graphics/fonts	PostScript, PDF, TrueType

Bitmaps and binary images

When we talk about bitmap images we are talking about a regular rectangular mesh of cells called pixels. Each pixel contains a colour value.

A pixel (the name comes from 'picture element') is the smallest change a computer can make to its display; it is a single dot.

Bitmaps contain two parameters: the number of pixels and the colour depth per pixel. Bitmaps are always arranged horizontally and vertically.

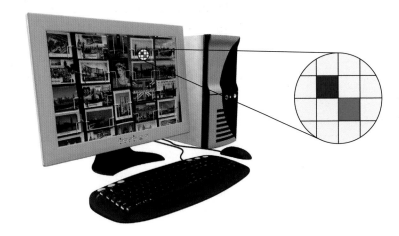

Pixels on a PC screen.

Pixels are usually defined as being square, although in practice their width-to-height ratio (aspect ratio) may vary.

Bitmaps are the main way of representing images on the computer.

Many, many pixels make up the computer's display. To give you some idea of what this means, the lowest resolution on a modern monitor is 640 × 480, which represents a grid of 640 pixels wide by 480 pixels high, or just over 300 000 pixels for the lowest resolution.

If we change the display settings to 1280 × 1024 we can fit many more pixels into the display. Because the monitor has not changed size, the pixels will become smaller, making everything on screen smaller but much better defined. The advantage of using higher resolutions is that smaller pixels let us display images with much more detail.

Colour depth

Although **colour depth** affects the amount of memory a picture requires, it does not affect the size at which the image is displayed but it has a major effect on the quality of the image. The term comes from the way a computer's display is made up. It can be visualised as a stacking series of 'bitplanes'. Imagine it as stacked panels of glass, some coloured, some clear. More depth means more panes of glass (that is, more bitplanes).

Each pixel in a bitmap contains colour information. The information content is always the same for all the pixels in a particular bitmap. The amount of colour information can vary according to the requirements of the application but there are some standards. Typical resolutions include 1-bit (black and white), 8-bit, 16-bit and 24-bit. To work out how many colours that is, simply calculate 2 to the power of the number of bits.

Key point

Pixels are the dots that make the image on screen. They are the smallest element of an image.

Key point

Resolution is the number of pixels or dots in an area, for example pixels per inch (ppi), sometimes referred to as dots per inch (dpi).

Question

How does the resolution of an image affect the size of the file?

Key term

Colour depth (or bit depth) refers to the number of bits used for each pixel or dot. The more bits there are, the more colours can be represented.

RGB

The RGB colour model is what is called an additive colour model. Red, green and blue light are added together in various ways to reproduce a broad array of perceived colours. The name of the model comes from the initials of the three additive primary colours: red, green and blue.

Unfortunately RGB is a device-dependent colour model: each separate device detects or reproduces a given RGB value differently. This is because the colour elements used (such as phosphors or dyes) respond to the individual red, green and blue levels differently from manufacturer to manufacturer, or even in the same device over time. An RGB value does not define the same colour across devices without some kind of colour management and this needs an alpha channel, which we will explore later.

1-bit monochrome (black and white)

One bit is the smallest possible information content that can be held for each pixel. Pixels with a 0 are referred to as black, and pixels with a 1 are referred to as white. Although only two states are possible, they are often interpreted not as black and white but as any two colours; 0 is mapped to one colour, 1 is mapped to another colour.

8-bit greys

Each pixel takes 1 byte (8 bits) of storage resulting in 256 different states. These states are mapped to a range of greys from black to white. The bitmap produced is referred to as a greyscale image.

The 0 is normally black and 255 white. The grey levels are the numbers in between, for example, in a linear scale 127 would be a 50% grey level.

0   255

A greyscale image showing 256 different states.

24-bit colour

Moving on from 8-bit grey we have 8 bits allocated to each of the primary colours of red, green and blue. In each colour, the value of 0 refers to none of that colour and 255 refers to fully saturated colour. Each component has 256 different states so there are 16 777 216 possible colours.

8-bit indexed colour

Indexed colour is a much more economical way of storing colour bitmaps without using three bytes per pixel. Each pixel has one byte associated with it. But the value in that byte is not a colour value but an index to a table of colours, called a palette or colour table.

If there are less than 256 colours in the image, the bitmap will be the same quality as a 24-bit bitmap but will be stored with one-third of the data.

Colour and animation effects can be achieved by simply modifying the palette. This immediately changes the appearance of the bitmap.

32-bit RGB

This is the same as 24-bit colour but with an extra 8-bit bitmap known as an alpha channel. This channel can be used to create masked areas or represent transparency.

How many colours?

A colour is created as a combination of four 8-bit values. The first value is referred to as alpha but it is mostly used internally. The second is called red, the third green and the fourth blue:

- alpha   7   6   5   4   3   2   1   0
- red   7   6   5   4   3   2   1   0
- green   7   6   5   4   3   2   1   0
- blue   7   6   5   4   3   2   1   0

Converted to decimal, each one of the red, green, and blue numbers would produce:

$$2^7 + 2^6 + 2^5 + 2^4 + 2^3 + 2^2 + 2^1 + 2^0$$

$$= 128 + 64 + 32 + 16 + 8 + 4 + 2 + 1$$

$$= 255$$

Therefore, each number has a value ranging from 0 to 255 in the decimal system. The alpha section is reserved for the operating system. The other three numbers are combined to produce a single value as shown in the diagram.

23	22	21	20	19	18	17	16	15	14	13	12	11	10	9	8	7	6	5	4	3	2	1	0
Blue								Green								Red							

Colour values for the RGB model.

Question

If an image has its colour depth decreased what is the effect?

Converted to decimal, this system can have a value of 255 × 255 × 255 = 16 581 375. This means that we can have approximately 16 million colours available.

Resolution

Resolution is necessary when visually viewing or printing bitmaps because pixels by themselves have no dimensions as they can vary in size on the screen according to the number of pixels displayed.

Resolution is normally specified in pixels per inch. Dots per inch (dpi) applies more to input and output devices, such as the printer or scanner, than to the screen display produced by your graphics card.

Suppose you use a screen resolution of 1024 × 768 pixels. The actual size of the display *as you see it* varies depending on how big your monitor is. Dots per inch comes into play as a measure more of image quality. The more dots per inch there are, the greater the detail that can be shown on the screen.

Key point

Pictures are stored in what is called metadata. This contains information about the image data that allows the computer to recreate the image from the binary data in the file. The metadata must contain the height and width in pixels and the colour depth in bits per pixel.

Question

What metadata is stored with an image file?

Colour depth conversion

Very often it is necessary to represent a bitmap with one colour depth on a device with different colour depth capabilities. If the new device has better colour than the bitmap, the bitmap can be represented exactly. But when the destination has lower capabilities, the bitmap has to be converted into something that gives the best possible representation.

There are a number of techniques that can be used. One popular technique is called dithering.

An image showing dithering and screening much enlarged.

Question

How many colours can be represented using a 4-bit colour depth?

There are other methods of converting bitmaps of high colour depth into those of lower colour depth but higher resolution. Such techniques are used in the printing industry and are called screening.

Difference between analogue and digital data

In the natural world everything is continuous and infinite. A number line is continuous, with values growing infinitely large and small. You can always come up with a number larger or smaller than any given number. The numeric space between any two integers is infinite. As an example, any number can be divided in half. But the world is not just infinite in a mathematical sense. The spectrum of colours is a continuous rainbow of infinite shades. Theoretically, you could always close the distance between you and your home by half, and you would never actually reach home.

Computers, on the other hand, are finite. Computer memory and other hardware devices have only so much room to store and manipulate data. In Computer Science we can only work towards representing enough of the world to satisfy our computational needs and our senses of sight and sound:

- Analogue data is continuous in the same way as the information that it represents. For example, a thermometer is an analogue device for measuring temperature. The liquid in a thermometer rises up the scale in proportion to the temperature rise. Computers cannot work with analogue information.
- Digital data breaks the information up into separate steps. This is done by breaking the analogue information into pieces and representing those pieces using binary digits.

We will explore the differences in more detail starting with the digital images we have just been studying.

Photographic images

At first, cameras used photographic film. An image is projected on to a sheet of photographic film (or paper) placed at the back of a light-tight box. The photographic film is coated on one side with light-sensitive chemicals (called an emulsion), which then record an analogue image of the scene viewed by the lens. Emulsion in the areas on the photographic paper that receive light undergo a chemical change and those areas not receiving light do not.

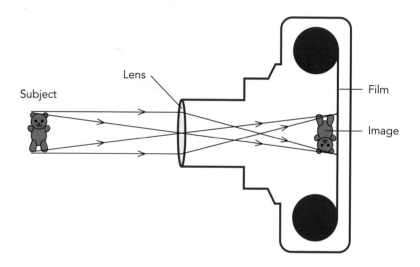

How an analogue film camera works.

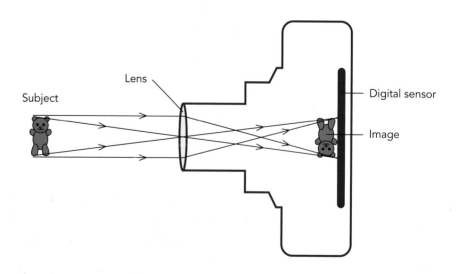

How a digital camera works.

In contrast, the process of taking a digital photograph is very different. A camera lens is used to focus the light from a scene not on to film but on to a silicon detector (a sensor circuit). The sensor surface is divided into a two-dimensional grid of pixels. The light intensity at each pixel (an analogue quantity) is sensed and converted to a multi-bit binary number.

Sound

The way that computers deal with sound has similarities to the way that they handle images. The bird sings in analogue not digital. The tone is infinite in its ability to carry. Original sound is analogue because that is how our ears work. But in order to turn this sound into something a computer can handle we need to create a digital sound wave that can be stored numerically.

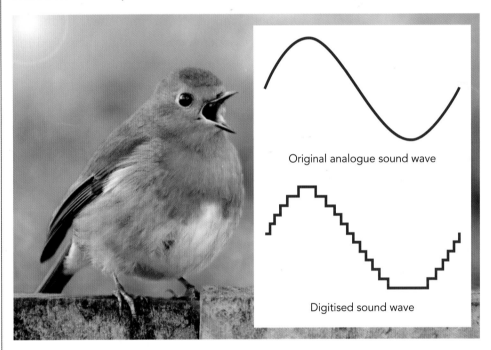

Original analogue sound wave

Digitised sound wave

Analogue and digital sound waves.

To compare digital and analogue sound, you need to look at a variety of factors.

Sample rate

In analogue recordings the tape recorder is recording any sound or noise that is coming through the microphones. In digital recording you don't have a constant recording, you have a series of samples or steps taken from the sound being recorded.

If you think about how animation works: a series of pictures are shown one after another to make it look like something is moving. In this case, digital recording takes a series of 'pictures' of what the sound is like and turns it into a digital recording.

Key point

The sample rate is the number of times the sound is sampled per second. It is measured in hertz (Hz) (100 Hz is 100 samples per second).

Question

How does the sample rate affect the quality of the playback for an MP3 sound track?

Key point

The bit rate is the space available for each sample, measured in kilobits per second.

Question

What effect does a high bit rate have on the number of sound files that can be stored on a CD?

Key term

A sensor is a device that can detect physical conditions, for example, temperature, weight, light and sound.

As with images, the more snapshots you have, the better the sound quality but at a higher cost of storage space.

Bits

By increasing the number of bits ('units of information') contained in the file, the amount of detail contained in each sample is increased. An example would be the sentence 'The large black cloud opened up, covering the ground with snow.' This contains more information than 'It snowed.' The more data, the more information you have. Imagine the detail that you can get from higher bit rates in your music.

Bit rate

Digital music files are measured by the amount of information that they can play per second, usually measured in kilobits per second (kbps or kbits/s). This is the amount of sound information presented to the listener every second.

Sound files played over an internet radio are 56 or 64 kbps to allow faster transport over networks. The standard for near-CD quality is 128 kbps, and some files go up to 320 kbps.

Temperature

You probably think that measuring temperature is not as important as dealing with sound and image files. But the measurement of temperature is critical to modern electronic devices. Laptop computers and other portable devices are densely packed with electronic hardware components that produce considerable energy in the form of heat. Knowledge of the system temperature can also be used to control battery charging as well as prevent damage to expensive microprocessors.

High-power portable equipment often has a cooling fan to maintain a correct working temperature. In order to conserve battery life, the fan should only operate when necessary. Accurate control of the fan requires a knowledge of critical temperatures from the appropriate temperature sensor.

A thermometer rises and falls in direct proportion to the temperature it measures.

The conversion from continuous analogue temperature data to digital data is similar to that of sound. Understanding bit rate is of vital importance.

11 Data storage and compression

Learning outcomes

- Understand and be able to convert between the following terms: bit, nibble, byte, kilobyte, megabyte, gigabyte and terabyte.
- Understand the need for data compression and methods of compressing data and that JPEG and MP3 are examples of lossy algorithms.
- Understand how a lossless, run-length encoding algorithm works.
- Understand that file storage is measured in bytes and that data transmission is measured in bits per seconds, and be able to calculate the time required to transmit a file and storage requirements for files.

Analogue and digital data

Computing systems can only store a limited amount of information, even if that limit is very large. To be able to fully understand data representation you need to first understand the differences between digital and analogue data. Analogue data is continuous in the same way as the information that it represents.

For example, a thermometer is an analogue device for measuring temperature. The liquid in a thermometer rises up the scale in proportion to the temperature rise. Computers cannot work with analogue information. Digital data breaks the information up into separate steps. This is done by breaking the analogue information into pieces and representing those pieces using binary digits.

Bits, nibbles and bytes

Bits, nibbles and bytes are small units of digital information:
- *bit*: a bit has a value of 1 or 0
- *nibble*: a nibble is 4 bits
- *byte*: a byte is 8 bits.

Bits are so small that we cannot use them for comparison from now on, so we use bytes instead.
- *kilobyte (KB)*: a kilobyte is 1024 bytes
- *megabyte (MB)*: a megabyte is 1 048 576 bytes or it is easier to remember as 1024 kilobytes
- *gigabyte (GB)*: a gigabyte is 1024 megabytes or 1 048 576 kilobytes
- *terabyte (TB)*: a terabyte is 1024 gigabytes or 1 048 576 megabytes
- *petabyte (PB)*: a petabyte is 1024 terabytes or 1 048 576 gigabytes
- *exabyte (EB)*: an exabyte 1024 petabytes or 1 048 576 terabytes

Key point

The magic number to remember is 1024.

Question

What is the mathematical difference between a megabyte and a terabyte?

■ *zettabyte (ZB)*: a zettabyte is 1024 exabytes or 1 048 576 petabytes

■ *yottabyte (YB)*: a yottabyte is 1024 zettabytes or 1 048 576 exabytes.

Just to give you an example of what these numbers all mean, if we stored photos of 3 MB in size on a hard drive with these memory volumes this would be the outcome:

Hard drive capacity	Number of 3 MB digital images that could be stored
1 kilobyte (KB)	None
1 megabyte (MB)	None
1 gigabyte (GB)	341
1 terabyte (TB)	349 525
1 petabyte (PB)	357 913 941
1 exabyte (EB)	366 503 875 925
1 zettabyte (ZB)	375 299 968 947 541
1 yottabyte (YB)	384 307 168 202 282 000

This assumes that our photos are only 3 MB in size. Professional cameras can produce RAW images that are over 100 MB in size. To achieve a photograph of 3 MB file size the image must be compressed.

Data compression

Run-length encoding

We now know that data must be compressed to work effectively on our mobile phones and portable computers. So now we need to learn how **data compression** works. Let's first look at a bitmap image; you will have learned about bitmap images in the last chapter.

Run-length encoding (RLE) is a data compression algorithm supported by most bitmap file formats, for example, TIFF, BMP and PCX.

RLE is suited for compressing any type of data, but the content of the data affects the compression ratio achieved by RLE. Let's explore what RLE is best suited to by looking at how it works. RLE works by reducing the physical size of a repeating string. This repeating string, called a *run*, is typically encoded into two bytes:

■ The first byte represents the number of characters in the run and is called the *run count*. In practice, an encoded run may contain 1 to 128 or 256 characters. The run count usually contains the number of characters minus one; this will be a value in the range of 0 to 127 or 255.

■ The second byte is the value of the character in the run, which is in the range of 0 to 255, and is called the *run value*.

Key term

Data compression is the reduction in file size to reduce download times and storage requirements.

Let's look at how this works in more detail. Uncompressed, a string character run of 20 characters:

XXXXXXXXXXXXXXXXXXXX

would require 20 bytes to store the string in its uncompressed form. The same string, after RLE encoding, would require only two bytes: 20X.

The 20X code generated to represent the character string is called an *RLE packet*.

In our example the first byte, 20, is the run count and contains the number of repetitions. The second byte, X, is the run value and contains the actual repeated value in the run.

It is a bit like going to a restaurant with 20 of your friends. If there are four things on the menu, the waitress will not write down a long list of 20 orders, she will simply write the menu items and put alongside them how many people want each item.

Bitmap storage

The most straightforward way of storing a bitmap is simply to list the bitmap information, byte after byte, row by row. Files stored by this method are often called RAW files. In a similar way, a new packet must be generated each time the run character changes, or each time the number of characters in the run exceeds the maximum count.

The following is a description of RLE, the simplest lossless compression technique, on a black and white image. This technique is best for bitmaps with only a few colours. Consider the following small, 17 × 10 pixel, 8-bit image of a Greek pi (π) symbol.

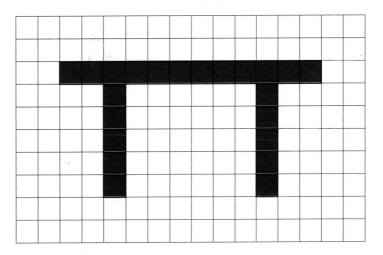

A simple bitmap image.

If this was to be stored in RAW form it would need 16 bytes per row for all 10 rows. The first two rows and the last two rows are the same level so it is much more efficient to simply save the number of same colours in a run along with the run colour. If we do this, the first two rows and the last two rows would need only two bytes for each row, not the full 16 bytes.

In RAW format this would be:

0	0	0	0	0	0	0	0	0	0	0	0	0	0	0	0
0	0	0	0	0	0	0	0	0	0	0	0	0	0	0	0
0	0	1	1	1	1	1	1	1	1	1	1	1	1	0	0
0	0	0	0	1	0	0	0	0	0	0	1	0	0	0	0
0	0	0	0	1	0	0	0	0	0	0	1	0	0	0	0
0	0	0	0	1	0	0	0	0	0	0	1	0	0	0	0
0	0	0	0	1	0	0	0	0	0	0	1	0	0	0	0
0	0	0	0	1	0	0	0	0	0	0	1	0	0	0	0
0	0	0	0	0	0	0	0	0	0	0	0	0	0	0	0
0	0	0	0	0	0	0	0	0	0	0	0	0	0	0	0

Using RLE, the first three rows would be:

16	0				
16	0				
2	0	12	1	2	0

While there are more details involved in the actual implementation of RLE than described here, this is the basic principle behind RLE of an image.

Text documents

Long runs are rare in certain types of data. For example, it is unlikely that our example of 20 X characters would occur in a typed document. In a standard ASCII document only a few words would even have two characters the same.

To encode a run in RLE requires a minimum of two characters' worth of information, as a run of single characters actually takes more space. Even data consisting entirely of two-character runs would remain the same size after RLE encoding. If only two of your friends go to the same restaurant, and each person orders a different menu item, there is no saving of time or space for the waitress to add how many people require each item.

But if we compare an ASCII document with a black and white image that is mostly white, such as a scanned page of a book, it will encode very well, due to the large amount of contiguous data that is all the same colour (white in this case). Anything with relatively few runs of the same colour will not work as well as images with large areas of the same colour.

Before we look at how to deal with images that do not lend themselves to this type of encoding, it is worth noting that different algorithms can store the RLE data in different ways. There are a number of variants of RLE.

In the sequential processing we have just looked at, a bitmap is encoded starting at the upper-left corner and proceeds from left to right across each scan line to the bottom-right corner of the bitmap. Each scan line is separated by a code to help put the image back together again. But alternatives to simply going from left to right do exist, such as those shown in the diagrams.

Encoding along the *x*-axis

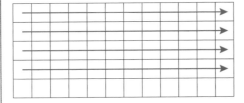

Zig-zag encoding

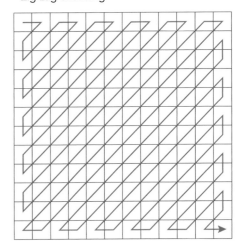

Encoding along the *y*-axis

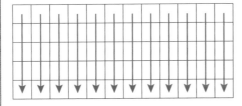

Encoding (4 × 4 pixel) tiles

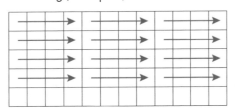

Run-length encoding variants

Lossless system of compression

So far we have seen how all the data in the string can be compressed without losing anything. The name for this type of algorithm is *lossless* – nothing is lost. But we also know that it will only work where data is repeated in the string. So what can we do with data which is not like this?

Lossy system of compression

If you take a photograph of a country view, large parts of the picture may look the same – the whole sky is blue and the grass is green, for example. But most of the individual pixels are a little bit different. The lossless system will not compress the file very well; it could even make the file larger. To make this picture smaller without compromising the resolution, you would have to change the colour value for certain pixels to make them the same before compression. If the picture had a lot of blue sky, the algorithm could pick one colour of blue that could be used for every pixel and replace all the variations with the same colour.

If the compression scheme works well, you would not notice the difference, but the file size could then be significantly reduced. You would simply lose, hence *lossy*, some of the more subtle differences. The more you lose, the better the compression.

It is not just in images where lossy compression is used. MP3 sound files use the same system, disregarding sounds that are similar and replacing them with continuous strings of the same sound data. Again, most listeners will never notice the difference, but to a connoisseur, MP3 could never replace live music or large, uncompressed sound files.

One of the main problems with lossy compression is that you cannot get the original file back after it has been compressed. You're stuck with the compression program's interpretation of the original. For this reason you cannot use this sort of compression for anything that needs to be reproduced exactly, including software applications or databases. Even professional photographers usually store their images in RAW uncompressed file formats as the quality is better, especially if they want to zoom in on the image. Sound studios work with uncompressed data before compressing it for sale.

For most uses, discarding data during the encoding process increases compression ratios without adversely affecting very complex images and sounds. For most of us this lossy algorithm works well both with real photographic images that contain lots of subtle variations in pixel values and for our favourite sounds. For this reason, one of the most popular image compression algorithms, JPEG, uses this lossy system of compression, as does MP3, one of the most popular sound compression algorithms.

So how does compression work with text?

For an easy-to-understand example, let's write a sentence:

'Run-length encoding makes files smaller; smaller files use run-length encoding.'

Now imagine this as a file. If each character and space in this sentence made up one unit of memory, the whole thing would have a file size of 79 bytes.

There are patterns in our sentence. Most words in the sentence appear twice. Only 'makes' and 'use' appear once. But to make use of this pattern we would need to create a dictionary, simply a way of cataloguing pieces of data, which in this case are words.

If we created a dictionary using a numbered index to represent each word, it could look something like this:

1. run
2. length
3. encoding
4. makes

5. files
6. smaller
7. use.

We could now write the sentence using our numbered index as:

1 2 3 4 5 6; 6 5 7 1 . 2 3

This new sentence has only 24 units. Therefore, the compressed file would have only 24 bytes of memory. In practice it would be a little larger as we would need to store our index alongside the data or it would be impossible to read the file, but you will have a good understanding of how this system could work.

The way in which actual compression algorithms work is a little more complicated than in our example. Most compression algorithms recognise other types of patterns.

An example of a more complex pattern in our sentence is how the letter 's' has a space after it in both 'files' and 'makes'. This is a pattern. But if there are not many instances in which a particular pattern occurs, the compression algorithm would probably overwrite it with a more apparent pattern. You can probably notice other patterns yourself, like how 'e' follows 'l' in four instances.

Most compression algorithms use patterns to compress a file. The patterns are also stored in what is called a dictionary.

Another way to compress text is to consider how often some words are used, words like 'the', 'and', 'which', 'that', 'is' and 'what'. If these words took up less space (that is, had fewer characters), the document would shrink in size. Even though the savings on each word would be small, they are used so often in a typical document that the combined savings would add up quickly. The name given to this technique is keyword encoding.

Representing video in data files

A moving image is a sequence of still images called frames which, when shown with very short time intervals between each frame, fools the brain into believing it is seeing a moving image. The brain smoothes over the change from one image to the next. With a minimum frame rate of around 20 frames per second needed to stop the moving image flickering, this takes a large number of images and a large amount of data to be stored in memory.

Computers handle two types of moving image: animations and videos (also called films, movies and video clips). The main difference between a video and animation is that with a video, images are captured using a camera. Animations are drawn images, not photographic images. Animations are often drawn with the help of a computer. The differences in programming terms are becoming blurred because videos are often heavily altered using computer techniques and animations used in computer games often look as lifelike as video images.

Video data compression

Let's say a full-colour image of 50 mm × 30 mm needs the 3 MB that our earlier images were. With 20 frames per second, a 5-minute video clip would need 300 seconds of images (5 minutes multiplied by 60 seconds per minute to get the total number of seconds).

To calculate the number of images needed, we need to multiply the number of seconds (300) by the number of images per second (20), giving us a total of 6000 images. Now we need to multiply the number of images by the size of each image (3 MB). We would therefore require 18 000 MB of storage space, almost 2 gigabytes of memory for a 5-minute video.

This video clip requires a large amount of memory, and if it is to be transferred via the internet we have a major issue. Even processing it in the computer's memory would need a very high-specification machine. We must use compression to make the film usable.

For moving images, a common compression technique is called MPEG (named after the Moving Picture Experts Group). MPEG is similar to JPEG for each of the frames in the sequence, but it performs further compression from one frame to the next by only recording the differences between the two frames. If in a scene someone has moved a leg slightly against an unchanging background it only records the change, not the background. It simply records that the background has not changed.

Understanding bandwidth

We have looked at file size and how images, sounds and text can be compressed using algorithms. But most data also needs to be communicated over wired and wireless networks. If you imagine a road network, the data size is the size of the vehicle or vehicle load which you wish to transport. But also important is the size of the roads, and in computer in terms this is called bandwidth.

What is bandwidth?

There are two very important points relating to bandwidth:

■ Bandwidth is a measure of the amount of data that can be transmitted through a connection over a given amount of time.

■ Bandwidth, also called data transfer rate, is usually expressed in bits per second (bps).

The amount of data transferred through a connection over time

For a rough calculation of how much bandwidth you might need, assume you have an image of 3 MB and it is downloaded once, then 3 MB of bandwidth is used. If that same 3 MB file is downloaded 10 times, then 30 MB of bandwidth is used.

Bandwidth or file transfer rate

Bandwidth is nearly the same as capacity. Every machine on the internet is connected either by a cable or through some other type of connection. This connection has a capacity to carry a certain amount of information through it, similar to our road system. This connection, like the road, may have a high or low capacity. If you compare a small street to a motorway, more cars can travel a mile on the motorway than on the small road.

The slowest of these capacities is the bandwidth; it is the fastest you can travel along the connection. Think of the connection as a long hose with someone pouring water into it at one end, and someone draining it out of the other. You cannot take out more than was put in, and if you pour it in too quickly the water will spill (losing data).

Data transmission

Data transmission, measured in bits per second (bps) or more normally kilobits per second (kbps), is called the baud rate or bit rate. It is the measure of bandwidth.

If a computer can receive 5 KB in a second, it would take 8 seconds for it to receive a file of 40 KB.

Bandwidth, however, is not measured in bytes, it is measured in bits. We know that 1 byte contains 8 bits. So, if a computer can receive 5 KB (5000 bytes) in 1 second, it can receive 40 000 bits per second: 5000 bytes × 8 bits = 40 000 bits per second or 40 kbps.

Before modern broadband connections, most people accessed the internet using dial-up modems. Let's look at a simple example of dial-up modem use. If a computer connects to the internet using a 56 kbps modem, in theory, it means that the computer could receive 56 000 bits per second (56 kbps). That would mean that the computer could receive about 7000 bytes per second. Remember that a byte equals 8 bits, so 56 000 bps + 8 bits = 7000 bytes. So, to receive the 20 KB image file, the 56 kbps dial-up connection would require slightly less than 3 seconds to receive the file (20 KB + 7000 bytes = 2.85 seconds).

Of course, in reality, just because the modem says that it can run at the speed does not mean that it actually will run at this speed. Usually the speed of connection is given at the maximum possible, not the average actual speeds achieved. Data connections are also often shared, just like our roads and motorways, and, just like a road, the more traffic the slower they become.

Streaming media file transmission

So far we have looked at quite small file sizes, but we know that a photographic image, however detailed, is much smaller than a video or animation file that requires lots of images.

When a video file is transmitted, frames are continuously delivered from the computer transferring the video to the computer playing it. Each frame is displayed as it is received. For example, consider a computer connected to the internet using a dial-up modem. If the modem is connected at 50 kbps, it could receive 5000 bytes (5 KB) of data per second. If each frame of the video was only 5 KB then the modem could only receive one frame per second (fps).

As we saw earlier, we need at least 20 fps; television is 30 fps. We also know that the more frames per second, the smoother the video playback appears to the viewer. So, a 1 fps video is a very slow and jumpy video.

With a higher bandwidth connection, more frames per second could be received. With a 128 kbps connection for example, 32 frames of 5 KB each could be delivered per second. But, a 5 KB image or frame is not very big. A small 320 × 200, 16-bit JPEG file can easily be 20 KB in size. So, for connection of 40 kbps of bandwidth, it would take 4 seconds to receive only one frame of the video! At that rate, the video would not be a video at all.

Frame rate, compression and bandwidth

We have our video and it has been compressed so that only the changes need to be sent. This compression means that frame rate may or may not have much of an effect on the bandwidth requirements of the video. If there is a great deal of change between frames, then the size of each frame image will be larger and more data must be transmitted for each frame. In this case, higher capture frame rates require increased bandwidth. But, if there is little or no change between frames, then little or no video data is transmitted for each frame. So, depending on the content of the compressed video, increasing the frame rate may have little or a great effect on how much bandwidth is required.

12 Encryption

Learning outcomes

- Understand the need for data encryption.
- Understand how a Caesar cipher algorithm works.

Algorithms in security

If you program anything that works over the internet and needs to handle confidential information you will have to use what are called **cryptographic** algorithms to keep the system secure.

Cryptographic algorithms are sequences of rules that are used to **encrypt and decipher** code. They are algorithms that protect data by making sure that unauthorised people cannot gain access to the data.

Most security algorithms involve the use of encryption, which allows two parties to communicate but uses coded messages so that third parties such as hackers cannot understand the communications.

Encryption algorithms are used to transform plain text into something unreadable. The encrypted data is then decrypted to restore it, making it understandable to the intended party.

There are hundreds of different types of cryptographic algorithms, but most fit into two classifications: they are either symmetric or asymmetric. Asymmetric algorithms use two keys: a public key and a private key.

The public key can be shared, but, to protect the data, the private key is only stored by the user. Encryption and decryption of data need both private and public keys. For example, data encrypted by the private key must be decrypted by the public key.

Symmetric algorithms are faster than asymmetric algorithms as one key is required. The disadvantage of this system is that both parties know the secret key.

Caesar cipher

Caesar **ciphers** are symmetric. There is one shared key. With a Caesar cipher, an algorithm replaces each letter in a message with a letter further along in the alphabet using a number key.

A Caesar cipher shifts the alphabet and is therefore also called a shift cipher. You also need a number key. The number key is simply the number of letters you need to shift.

The Caesar cipher is one of the oldest types of ciphers. It is named after Julius Caesar, the Roman emperor, who is said to have used it to send messages to his generals over 2000 years ago.

Let's look at an example with a shift key of 1.

Riddle: What is the clumsiest bee?
Answer: b cvncmjoh cff

The deciphered answer: a bumbling bee.

Question

If a shift key of 2 has been used, decipher the following Caesar cipher: gzco swguvkqp.

(Answer = exam question.)

Each letter in the encrypted message is just the next letter along in the alphabet because the key is 1. If we look at this mathematically the encryption formula is:

$E_n(x) = (x + n) \bmod 26$.

And here is decryption formula:

$D_n(x) = (x - n) \bmod 26$.

The alphabet we are working with contains 26 letters and n is a number less than or equal to 25.

These assumptions can be modified for any alphabet language of your choice. If the alphabet contains m letters, then n has to be less than or equal to $m - 1$.

Here is a general outline and picture of how the algorithm works. You should be aware that for our example here the key n is set to 3, but it will work with any number.

1. Assign numeric values to each letter in the alphabet.
2. Encrypt:
- for each letter in plain_text
  - new letter is letter_numeric_value + n

3. Decrypt:

- ■ for each letter in cipher
  - ■ plain_text_letter is letter_numeric_value – n

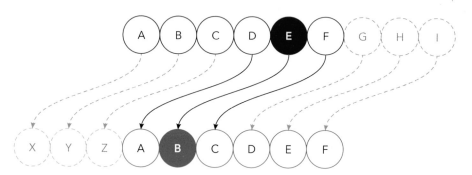

A cipher with a key of 3.

To create an encrypted text we need to create a shift. Ask the user for the number key:

- ■ create shift.

Ask the user for the text to convert:

- ■ convert string
- ■ create index.

Calculate the new letter:

- ■ index + shift.

We also need to consider what happens if the index + shift is past the letter Z. In this instance we need to return to the start of our alphabet by deducting the length of the alphabet.

Let's look at how this simple cipher could work in Python 3:

```python
import string

def createShift(shift,convert):
    alphabet = string.ascii_lowercase
    finished = ''

    for char in convert:
        if char in alphabet:
            for index, alphChar in enumerate(alphabet):
                if char is alphChar:
                    if index+shift < len(alphabet):
                        finished += alphabet[index+shift]
                    else:
                        finished += alphabet[(index + shift) -
                        (len(alphabet))]
```

```
                break
       else:
            finished += char
    return finished


if __name__ == '__main__':
    shift = int(input('What is the shift key? '))
    convert = input('What text would you like to convert? ').lower()

    print('\n' + createShift(shift,convert) + '\n')
```

Note how the programmer has forced the user input into lower-case ASCII.

Task

Write an algorithm in your chosen programming language to create and decode a Caesar cipher. The user should enter the key and the text.

13 Databases

Learning outcomes

- Understand the characteristics of structured and unstructured data.
- Understand that data can be decomposed and organised in a structured database.
- Understand the need for and be able to use SQL statements.

Database characteristics

All businesses have data that needs to be gathered, collated and analysed, and a relational database satisfies these needs. Let's first explore what a database does.

Databases use a series of tables to store data. A table simply refers to a two-dimensional representation of data stored in rows and columns. For example:

Steve	Cushing	steve@example.com
John	Wilson	john@example.com
Jess	Hadden	jess@example.com

So we have a table with rows containing a person's details and columns.

First, each table needs a unique name so that the database management system (often referred to as the DBMS) can find the right table. We will call this table 'contacts'.

Next, each column needs a name.

first_name	last_name	email_address
Steve	Cushing	steve@example.com
John	Wilson	john@example.com
Jess	Hadden	jess@example.com

To make the database usable we need to add a unique key to the table. Most database developers create their own column with a computer-generated unique number to act as the unique key. This is referred to as the database's key field.

first_name	last_name	email_address	key
Steve	Cushing	steve@example.com	1001
John	Wilson	john@example.com	1002
Jess	Hadden	jess@example.com	1003

Question

Data handling applications usually work through a DBMS. What is a DBMS and why is it used?

Key term

A database consisting of only one table is called a **flat file database**.

We could just keep adding fields for any additional data. This would be called a **flat file database**, but these can be very slow, so most professional databases have different tables linked together. Let's look at how that works.

Let's imagine that each of the people in the table buys a product from an online shop. The company produces a table of sales information.

number	product_name	product_code	item_id
10	Rise and Fall	B607	1001
2	Times Square	H766	1002
1	Home	L678	1003

Now we need to link the two tables together, to relate the data in one table with the other. This is where the relational database gets its name.

item_id	key
1001	1001
1002	1002
1003	1003

So, by referring to the linking table you can see that Jess Hadden purchased one copy of the product L678 'Home'.

You are probably wandering why the *item_id* and *key* are the same. What happened to the unique key field? In relational databases nothing is unique in combined tables. The second key is called a foreign key, which means that the number used in a foreign key column is not necessarily unique to the linked table, but it must be unique to the table it is referring to.

In addition to the comprehensive functionality of a relational database, there is a need not only to develop but also to maintain the database. IT personnel, such as data analysts, database designers and database administrators, all need the ability to modify the data within a database to produce useful information for both day-to-day organisational activities and long-term planning.

Databases are like spreadsheets ... aren't they?

Most of us are familiar with spreadsheets. We find them simple to create and they are often used in schools in the same way as a database, but is this entirely correct? Let's analyse the features and functionality of spreadsheets to investigate how good a database tool they actually are.

In a similar way to databases, spreadsheets are frequently used to capture and store information in tables. They have the capability to link table cells on one worksheet to those on another worksheet, and they can specify that data be entered in a particular cell in a particular format. It is also a simple operation to calculate formulas from a group of cells on the spreadsheet, create charts and process data in other ways.

Having said this, there are many areas in which spreadsheets are nothing like a database and the following table highlights this.

Spreadsheets	Databases
Cells can be formatted as a formula	Database columns have a fixed value
A number of different data types can be stored in a column of a spreadsheet	In a column of a database only a single data type can be stored
Accessible to only one user at any one time	Accessible to a multiple of users at any time as well as offering a choice of 'read and write' permissions across various areas of a database
Corrupted spreadsheets cannot usually be repaired	There is a range of tools for repairing databases
No way of making a row (record) unique	Individual rows within databases have the capability to be identified by a unique 'primary key'

Relational databases

As we have seen, a relational database is a group of data items assembled into a set of formatted tables from which data can be searched, accessed and interrogated in a multitude of different ways without having to reorganise the database tables.

The standard user interface to any relational database is the structured query language (SQL). By using SQL statements, interactive queries for information can be made for the purpose of retrieving information from a relational database and for gathering data for reports.

As well as being quite simple to create and access, a relational database has the significant benefit of being relatively straightforward to extend. After the original database has been produced, a new data category can be included without the need to modify all the existing applications as new tables can be added and linked.

As mentioned, relational databases are a set of tables consisting of data organised into predefined categories. The tables, which are sometimes referred to as *relations*, comprise one or more categories that are arranged into columns. Each row contains a unique instance of data for the categories defined by the columns.

Databases can be designed so that different users see a personalised view of the database that is customised to suit the user's needs. For example, a sales manager may wish to view a report on all customers who had bought products after a certain date, whereas a finance manager within the same company could, from the same database, obtain a report on accounts that needed to be paid. This is achieved by simply relating the tables needed by that user.

Components of relational databases

The foundation for any relational database management system (RDBMS) is the relational model and this has three basic components:

- a store
- a method of creating and retrieving data
- a method of ensuring that the data is logically consistent.

Let's look at the fundamental components of a traditional relational database system and how it is designed.

Tables

A table in a relational database is also referred to as a 'relation'. It is a two-dimensional structure used to store related information. A relational database consists of two or more related tables.

Records

In databases, **records** are a complete single set of information. Records are comprised of fields (see later). A set of records constitutes a file. For example, a personnel file of employees may contain records that have seven fields, such as age, gender, house number, street name, town, telephone number, National Insurance number and so on.

Rows

A row within a 'relation' table is an instance of one record, such as one employee and his or her respective details that are contained within the fields of the records (see later).

Columns

Columns within a database table contain all the information of a single type, such as all the employees' names, all the phone numbers or all the address details. As part of the validation and verification of the information, columns are usually formatted to accept certain types of data such as integers, Boolean, decimals (to a stated number of decimal places) or strings.

> **Key term**
>
> A **record** is all the data about one item in a database.

Fields

Within relational database tables, a **field** is a single snippet of data that is at the intersection of a row and a column. It is the smallest piece of information that can be retrieved using the database's SQL and forms part of an individual record.

Queries

A database query is fundamentally a question that you put to the database. The outcome of the query is the information that is returned by the database in answer to the question. Queries are created using SQL, which looks like a high-level programming language.

Primary keys

Every relational database should contain one or more columns that are assigned as the primary key. The important and crucial fact for the primary key to work is that the value it holds must be unique for each of the records contained within the table.

If we take our personnel database example referred to earlier, we know that it contains personal information on all our organisation's employees. Now, we need to choose a suitable column of information, where each field within that column can uniquely identify each employee's record, which can act as our primary key. So why don't we choose the column containing the employee's surname?

Well, this would not work correctly because there may be two or more people working within the business called Jones, Patel or Smith, for example. The same problem would occur if we used the column containing first names or street titles. You could use National Insurance numbers; however, their use is controversial because of certain privacy issues. A better idea would be to create a column with unique employee identifiers and, these days, this is what most employers do.

When the primary key has been selected and built into the database, the database management system will ensure the uniqueness of the key, so that should you attempt to add a duplicate record with a key that already exists within the table, the system will disallow the addition and present you with a warning window.

Relationships

Database relationships work by comparing data in key fields. This occurs between fields that have corresponding names in both tables. In almost all cases, the fields contain the primary key for one of the tables, which then supplies the unique identifier for each record and the 'foreign' key in the other table. The foreign key is a column identified to establish a connection between the data in two tables.

A link is established between two tables by adding the column that holds the primary key in the first table to the other table. The duplicated column within the second table then becomes the foreign key.

Although the most important responsibility of a foreign key is to manage the data that is stored in the foreign key table, it additionally manages changes to data in the primary key table. The link between the two tables confirms that data integrity is maintained between the two tables by ensuring that alterations cannot occur to data in the primary key table, if the alterations undermine the link to the data in the foreign key table.

If someone tries to delete the record row in a primary key table or to alter a primary key value, an error will occur if it is linked to a foreign key value in another table. In order to carry out a successful alteration or deletion to a record in a foreign key table, initially, you should either delete or alter the foreign key data contained within the second table, therefore linking the foreign key to different primary key data.

Indexes

Database indexes assist database management systems to find and sort records more quickly. It is really important that when you produce a database, you should also create indexes for the columns used in queries to find data.

Indexes in databases can be compared to indexes in books. If you look at a book's index, it enables you to find information quickly without having to read through the entire book. Within a database, the index enables the database software to search for and find data in a table without having to scan the whole table.

Indexes can be based on a single field or on a multiple of fields. Indexes that use a number of fields enable the user to distinguish between records in which the first field may have the same value.

Even though indexes greatly improve the efficiency of a database, tables that possess indexes need more storage space within the database. Also, the commands that insert, update or delete data within databases need more processing time.

When choosing the fields to use for indexes you should consider using fields that you search frequently, fields that you sort regularly or fields that you combine frequently with fields in other tables when queries are created. If a large number of the values within a field are identical, then an index may not significantly improve the speed of queries.

Structured query language (SQL)

All SQL code is written in the form of a query statement and this is 'executed' against a database.

SQL queries perform some type of data operation, which could be selecting, inserting/updating or creating what are called data objects.

Every query statement begins with a clause such as DELETE, CREATE, SELECT or UPDATE.

Creating a table

To create the table we looked at earlier in this chapter using SQL, we need to create a table called contacts with first_name, last_name and email_address plus a key.

The SQL command for creating a table is easy: it is CREATE TABLE. So our code would look like this:

```
CREATE TABLE contacts (
   first _ name  CHAR  (30)  NULL ,
   last _ name  CHAR  (40)  NULL ,
   email _ address  VARCHAR  (80)  NULL
   key  INT  IDENTITY (1001, 1)  NOT NULL ,
   );
```

If you look at the code most of it should make sense to you.

We are stating that first_name is a character column (CHAR) that will store 30 or fewer characters. We are also saying the first_name can be empty using the NULL statement. The last_name field is similar but can have 40 characters.

The email_address field uses VARCHAR to store a set of alphanumeric characters in a variable string. We could have used CHAR but this command allocates memory space to the stated length, so the last_name command will allocate 40 spaces even if the last name is really short. In some, but not all systems, the VARCHAR will use less memory as it is a variable and will only store the number of characters used. I say *some* systems because there could be a minimum length.

The line for the key uses the term INT as we want it to be an integer. The next section of code shows that we want it to start with 1001 and go up in

Question

What type of business software lets users query data and generate forms?

---

increments of 1. Notice also the use of NOT NULL as we must have a key number to make our relational database work.

The semicolon at the end of a statement tells the database system that you have finished the command.

Now we have a table but so far it has no data. To add data we need to use the command INSERT INTO.

The SQL INSERT INTO statement

The SQL INSERT INTO statement is used to insert a new row in a database table. Let's have a look at the syntax of the function. There are two methods of writing the INSERT INTO statement. In the first method, we do not specify the column names where the data will be inserted, only their values:

```
INSERT INTO table_name
VALUES (value1, value2, value3,...)
```

In the second method, both the column names and the values to be inserted are specified:

```
INSERT INTO table_name (column1, column2, column3,...)
VALUES (value1, value2, value3,...)
```

So we have our table called contents and we know how to insert data. Now let's add the first record:

```
INSERT INTO contacts (first_name,
    last_name,
    email_address)
  VALUES ('Steve',
    'Cushing',
    'steve@example.com');
```

You must add data in the same order as the rows in your table. If you do not know the data, for example Steve Cushing does not have an email address, you would add NULL:

```
INSERT INTO contacts (first_name,
    last_name,
    email_address)
  VALUES ('Steve',
    'Cushing',
    NULL);
```

The SQL UPDATE statement

What happens if a user changes his or her email address? What we need to do is UPDATE the field. The UPDATE statement is used to edit existing records in a table. Let's take a look at the syntax of the UPDATE statement:

```
UPDATE table _ name
SET column1=value, column2=value2,...
WHERE some _ column=some _ value
```

It is worth taking note of the WHERE clause, which specifies which record or records should be updated. If the WHERE clause is left out, then all records will be edited.

Let's change Steve Cushing's email address in our database:

```
UPDATE contacts
    SET email _ address = 'scushing@example.org'
WHERE contact _ id = 1001;
```

Notice the use of the SET command: this changes a row in the database table. You can add lots of changes to a row in the database using the SET command if you separate each column change with a comma.

Other important commands

The SELECT command is used to tell the database system what you want to find in a table, but you must say which data you want from a column. If you want all the columns you would use SELECT *.

In SQL, the SELECT statement is used to choose data from a database. Let's have a look at the syntax of the statement:

```
SELECT column _ name(s)
FROM table _ name
```

and

```
SELECT * FROM table _ name
```

WHERE commands select only the data stated in the command, so:

```
SELECT first _ name, email _ address
    FROM contacts
    WHERE first _ name = 'Steve';
```

will only find people with the first_name Steve.

Sorting

What if we want to sort the data in our database?

```
SELECT *
  FROM contacts
  ORDER BY last_name DESC;
```

will sort the data by last_name in DESCending order.

Deleting

What if we want to delete a customer in our data table?

```
DELETE FROM contacts
WHERE key = 1003;
```

DELETE removes the row in table 'contacts' where the 'key' is equal to 1003. That means Jess Hadden will no longer be in our database.

The table shows some of the other commands used by SQL databases.

Operator	The operator compare data
=	to see if it is equal
<>	to see if it is not equal
<	to see if the data is less than your criteria
<=	to see if the data is less than or equal to your criteria
>	to see if the data is greater than your criteria
>=	to see if the data is greater than or equal to your criteria
IS NULL	to make sure that there is no data in the column

What is structured data?

Structured data is data or information displayed in titled columns and rows that can easily be ordered and processed. So far in this chapter we have looked at structured data in databases. It can be compared to a perfectly organised filing cabinet where everything is identified and labelled, making data very easy to find.

What is unstructured data?

Unstructured data is usually binary data, which has no identifiable structure. It can be compared to having a single drawer for all your clothes, socks, shirts and so on, all mixed together.

A process of organisation needs to take place (through the use of specialised software or algorithms) so that the items can then be searched through and categorised (to an extent).

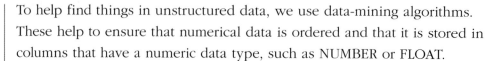

To help find things in unstructured data, we use data-mining algorithms. These help to ensure that numerical data is ordered and that it is stored in columns that have a numeric data type, such as NUMBER or FLOAT.

Categorical data is identified by category or classification and is then stored in columns that have a character data type, such as CHAR.

Of course, there is also unstructured data that is not numerical, including things such as web pages, document libraries, PowerPoint presentations and emails.

We live in a world where we're digitising everything and sharing it across the internet with our personal social media connections …. It's all unstructured data that doesn't fit the relational structured data model.

Extracting meaningful information from unstructured data is a critical part of modern computer science.

Topic 4
COMPUTERS

14 Machines and computational models

Learning outcomes

- Understand the concept of a computer as a hardware machine or as a virtual machine.
- Understand that there is a range of computational models.
- Understand the input–process–output model.

The input–process–output model

A computer can be described using a simple model:

- The *input* stage represents the flow of data into the process from outside the system.
- The *processing* stage includes all tasks required to make a transformation of the inputs.
- The *output* stage is where the data and information flow out of the transformation process.
- The *storage* stage keeps data when the computer is switched off.

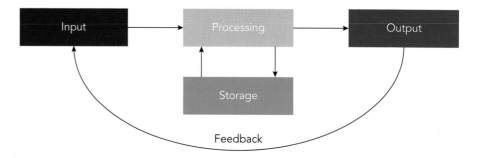

A computer considered as an input–process–output model.

Sequential algorithms

In computer science, a sequential algorithm is an algorithm that is executed sequentially, one step at a time from start to finish. It does this without any other processing execution. Most standard computer algorithms are sequential.

Parallel algorithms

In computer science, a parallel algorithm is an algorithm that can be executed a piece at a time on many different processing devices, and then combined at the end to get the correct result.

Many parallel algorithms are executed concurrently, in other words at the same time, although in general the term concurrent algorithm is a distinct computer science concept. Because of this, it is best to try to understand which aspect of an algorithm is parallel and which is also concurrent.

Non-parallel, non-concurrent algorithms are often referred to as 'sequential algorithms', in contrast to concurrent algorithms.

When studying parallel algorithms you will probably also come across the term multi-agent computing.

Multi-agent

Multi-agents do not have to be on different machines; they could be multiple processes on a single chip or machine. What is important to note is that they act without centralised control; they do their separate jobs before coming together to compare results.

Multi-agent systems are often used in artificial intelligence. They simplify problem solving by dividing the necessary knowledge into separate parts and then give each part to an independent intelligent agent. Computer scientists call this distributed artificial intelligence. It is not just in artificial intelligence that multi-agent systems are used. Distributed algorithms have been widely studied in computer science and they can be found in game theory, economics, operations research, logic, philosophy and linguistics programming.

As an agent is anything that can perceive its environment through sensors and act on that environment through actuators, most modern robotic systems are also multi-agent systems.

You need to be careful not to confuse single-agent systems with multi-agent systems. In multi-agent systems, the control is typically distributed. This means that there is no central process that collects information from each agent and then decides what action each agent should take. The decision making of each agent lies to a large extent within the agent itself.

Virtual machines

To understand what a virtual machine is, we must first look at what is meant by a machine. If we look at our input–process–output model, a machine is the hardware processing a program. The machine consists of a logical memory **address** that has been assigned to a process, along with the user-level registers and instructions that allow the execution of code belonging to the process.

Key term

The **address** is a location in main memory used to store data or instructions.

The input and output (I/O) part of the machine is accessible from the operating system, and the only way the process can interact with the I/O system is by operating system calls within the processing part of the system. Processes are created and executed over a set period of time.

From the perspective of the operating system, the entire system is supported by the underlying machine. The machine is a full execution environment that can simultaneously support a number of processes potentially belonging to single or multiple users. All these processes share a file system and other I/O resources.

Any virtual machine is a combination of a real machine and virtualising software. The virtual machine (called a guest) is a further abstraction from the hardware and may even have resources different from the real machine. For example, a virtual machine may have more or fewer processors than the real machine, and the processors may execute a different instruction set than the real machine does.

It is important to note that often a virtual machine provides less performance than an equivalent real machine running the same software due to the extra level of abstraction.

Types of virtual machines

Whole-system virtual machines

Whole-system virtual machines are more dynamic and more complex than any other type of virtual machine. They are sometimes referred to as hardware virtual machines. Whole-system virtual machines provide a complete system platform in order to support the running and the execution of a complete operating system. To implement a system virtual machine of this type, the virtual machine software must emulate the entire hardware environment. It must control the emulation of all the instructions and convert the guest system operations to equivalent operating system calls.

This allows for the sharing of physical information and physical machine resources between different virtual machines operating on the same system, as they are each technically running their own operating system.

The advantage of system virtual machines is that the user can have multiple virtual machines operating on the same computer and they run completely independently. The main disadvantage is that a virtual machine is less efficient than a real machine as it accesses the hardware indirectly.

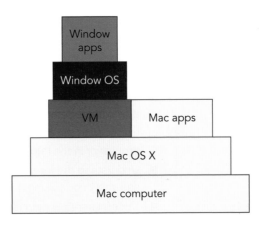

Using a virtual machine (VM) it is possible to run Windows and Windows applications on a Mac computer.

Process virtual machines

Process virtual machines are simpler to operate. Process virtual machines are designed to support only a single process and run just a single program as opposed to the more complete system platform provided by the whole-system virtual machines.

Process virtual machines are also called application virtual machines. Their main purpose is to provide a programming environment independent of a platform which can take details from an underlying operating system or hardware, and to allow a single program to execute its tasks in the same way as it would on a regular platform.

The simplest example of this is often not noticed as a virtual machine. If more than one user has his or her own account on a computer they each have, in effect, a virtual machine.

15 Hardware

Learning outcomes

- Understand the function of hardware components of a computer system and how they work together.
- Understand the concept of a stored program and the role of components of the processor in the fetch–decode–execute cycle.
- Understand the function of assembly code and be able to interpret a block of assembly code using a given set of commands.
- Understand how data is stored on physical devices.
- Understand how microcontrollers can be programmed to control actuators and take input from sensors.

Hardware components of a computer

Hardware is the name given to a collection of physical 'things' that when put together in a certain way form a 'system'. The hardware is the machine. You must understand the function of the hardware components of a computer to be able to write programs.

The human body could be considered as a collection of hardware. First, you have your brain, not the thought processes that go on inside it, but the physical organ. Then you have the internal hardware that keeps your body working such as your heart, lungs and digestive system.

You also have 'devices' for taking on board different information such as the eyes for visual data, your hands that use the sense of touch for tactile information, your ears for sound information and your tongue for a sense of taste.

All this information is processed and stored in your brain while you are still alive.

Your body has ways of outputting information too. This involves using speech as well as movements, expressions and gestures that you can make with your face and body.

Hardware refers to parts or components of a system that can be physically touched (although there are not many of us that could truly say that they would like to touch someone's brain).

Let's now take a look at the hardware components of a computer and how they fit together to form a system. The main components are:

- the **central processing unit** (CPU)
- memory, such as random access memory modules

- storage devices, such as hard disk drives
- input devices, such as mice and keyboards
- output devices, such as monitors and printers
- communication devices, such as network cards and modems.

For these components to work together they must be connected using a **motherboard**.

Motherboard

Motherboards link the CPU to the memory and other hardware.

A motherboard from inside a PC.

The motherboard could be compared to human nerves – the essential connections that send and receive signals throughout your body. The CPU computes data and uses the motherboard to receive and send signals to devices such as the hard disk drive (storage). The motherboard is also responsible for holding settings such as the time and date. As with the CPU, motherboards have speeds, called the bus speed.

A **bus** is the circuit that connects one part of the motherboard to another. The more data the motherboard's bus can handle at any one time, the faster the system. The speed of the bus is measured in megahertz (MHz). Motherboards have many buses; each one transfers data from one computer component to another.

Key term

The motherboard is a central printed circuit board that holds all the crucial hardware components of the system and enables them to work together.

Key term

The bus is a part of a computer's architecture that transfers data and signals between all the components of the computer.

Within a computer system there are basically two types of hardware:

- the hardware within the system consisting of the CPU, which is situated on the motherboard
- the hard disk drive, the random access memory, optical drive and other circuit boards such as the graphics and sound cards.

These are all regarded as hardware because if you removed the PC's case you could physically touch the devices. Do *not* do that unless you know what you are doing as you could put yourself and others at risk.

Question ❓

What is the purpose of the CPU?

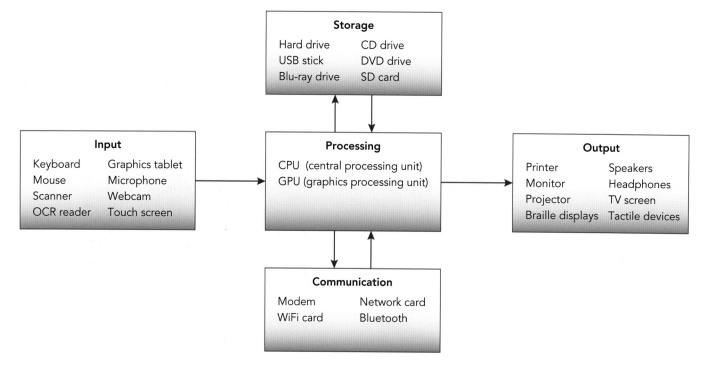

A summary of a computer system's hardware.

Question ❓

Define a system.

The function of hardware components inside a computer

The storage of instructions in a computer's memory enables the computer to perform a variety of tasks either in sequence or occasionally. The stored program concept is a technical process with four key subcomponents all working together.

The process that moves information through the subcomponents is called the 'fetch–execute' cycle, and we will look at this later in the chapter. Program instructions are normally executed in sequential order.

One of the four essential subcomponents that make computers function is the control unit. The control unit is part of the CPU and it drives the fetch–execute cycle. The other key components are:

- memory (four types of memory are used: RAM, ROM, registers and others, such as cache)
- input/output (I/O)
- arithmetic logic unit.

We will look at RAM (random access memory) and ROM (read-only memory) later in this chapter but there is a third key type of memory in every computer: registers. Register cells are powerful and costly, and are always physically located close to the heart of computing. Among the registers, several of them are the main participants in the fetch–execute cycle.

Central processing unit (CPU)

The brain of the computer is the CPU. It receives information from sensors and communicates this to the output devices using a bus. In a similar way, your body receives information from your eyes and ears as electrical signals transmitted not by a bus but through the nervous system. Your body has ways of outputting information: speech, movements, expressions and gestures. Our main memory is part of the brain.

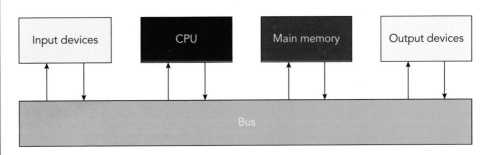

The CPU (computer's brain) is connected to the other hardware components by a bus.

Just like our brain, the CPU's purpose is to process data. It does this by performing functions such as searching and sorting data and calculating and decision-making using the data. For every task that you carry out on a computer, whether it is designing a spreadsheet, writing an email, playing a game or searching the internet, all of the data-processing associated with those and many more tasks is carried out by the CPU.

The history of the CPU is very interesting. At the heart of a CPU is what is called the processor. Its name tells you what it does. The first CPU chip was invented in 1971. It was basically a 4-bit processor designed for a calculator. Its instructions were 8 bits long. Program and data were separate. Since these early days of CPUs with single-core processors there have been many changes to the 'brain' in our computers.

Key point

The CPU is the 'brain' of the computer. If you did not have the CPU, you would not have a computer.

Processor speeds have doubled every few years. The first big change to the CPU was the addition of a second processor called a dual-core processor. Each processor has its own cache and controller. The benefit of this is that each processor functions as efficiently as a single processor. Because the two processors are linked together, they can perform operations twice as fast as a single processor.

Imagine that you have to make a breakfast of buttered toast and a cup of tea. However fast you work, some things need your full attention. You cannot butter the toast and pour the tea at the same time. But imagine that you had a second person to help. If they made the toast and you made the tea the process would be much faster.

A photograph of a modern quad-core processor. How many processors would this chip have?

Technology has not stopped at dual-core processors. The next step was quad-core processors, followed by hexa-core processors (containing six cores). Some computers even have octa-core processors (eight cores). You may be thinking that each addition multiplies the processing power of a single-processor machine, but it does not always work like this. The software running on the machine has to be designed to take full advantage of the processor.

The CPU undertakes the instructions it receives from programs in what is called a cycle. If we go back to the example of making the toast and tea, if you worked faster you could produce the breakfast quicker. Perhaps the addition of a kettle that boiled water faster would help too. The CPU not only has a number of cores, it also has speed. The speed of the CPU is

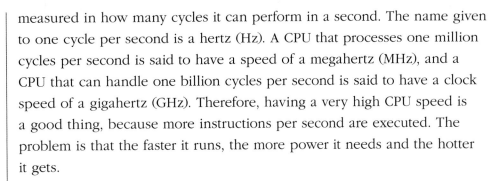

measured in how many cycles it can perform in a second. The name given to one cycle per second is a hertz (Hz). A CPU that processes one million cycles per second is said to have a speed of a megahertz (MHz), and a CPU that can handle one billion cycles per second is said to have a clock speed of a gigahertz (GHz). Therefore, having a very high CPU speed is a good thing, because more instructions per second are executed. The problem is that the faster it runs, the more power it needs and the hotter it gets.

Most computer users cannot notice the speed differences between one processor and the next, unless they are playing the very latest computer games. And if we go back to our breakfast analogy, however fast you work and however many friends you have to help you, if the instructions are not clear and the items you need are not available, you will not be any faster making breakfast. With CPUs, programmers have a part to play in maximising the speed.

Logic and the CPU

We looked at the purpose of the CPU earlier in this chapter but it also contains the following components:

- a **control unit** which fetches, decodes and executes instructions
- an arithmetic logic unit (ALU) which performs arithmetic and logical operations on data
- registers: fast, on-chip memory which is dedicated or general purpose
- an internal clock derived directly or indirectly from the system's clock
- internal buses to connect the components
- logic gates to control the flow of information.

Registers are storage locations within the circuitry of the CPU. They are very fast on-chip memory storing binary values using 32 or 64 bits. Information is held there while it is being interpreted or manipulated. Remember that the second essential component in any system is memory. Let's now take a more detailed look at how the control unit and the fetch–decode–execute cycle works.

Fetch–decode–execute cycle

The fetch–decode–execute cycle is sometimes called the instruction cycle or fetch–execute cycle.

A program first fetches an instruction from the counter/control unit in the processor. Next, the processor copies this information to the main memory. The information is sent to the memory buffer register by way what is called a data bus. Finally, the instructions are copied to the current

Key term

The control unit works with the CPU to control the flow of data within a computer system.

instruction register for decoding and execution. The decoder interprets the instruction. The decode cycle is used for interpreting the instruction that was fetched in the fetch cycle.

Let's look at each of these steps in more detail. The process starts with the address in memory of the first instruction being stored in the **program counter**.

Fetch the next instruction

The program counter contains the address of the next instruction to be executed, so the control unit goes to the address in memory specified in the program counter, makes a copy of the contents and places the copy in the instruction register. At this point the instruction register contains the instruction to be executed. Before going on to the next step in the cycle, the program counter must be updated to hold the address of the next instruction to be executed when the current instruction has been completed. Because the instructions are stored contiguously in memory, adding 1 to the program counter puts the address of the next instruction into the program counter. So the control unit increments the program counter up 1.

Accessing memory takes one cycle. Most computers can access memory at least 133 million cycles per second (1.33 MHz), so one access takes 7.5 billionths of a second.

Decode the instruction

In order to execute the instruction in the instruction register, the control unit has to determine what the instruction is. It might be an instruction to access data from an input device, to send data to an output device or to perform some operation on a data.

At this phase, the instruction is decoded into what are called control signals. The logic of the circuitry in the CPU determines exactly which operation is to be executed. The instructions themselves are built into the circuits. This is why a computer can only execute instructions that are expressed in machine language.

Get data if needed

It may be that the instruction to be executed requires additional memory accesses in order to complete its task.

Execute the instruction

Once an instruction has been decoded and any operands (data) fetched, the control unit is ready to execute the instruction. Execution involves sending signals to the **ALU** to carry out the processing. In the case of adding a number to a register, the operand is sent to the ALU and added to the contents of the register. When the execution is complete, the cycle begins again.

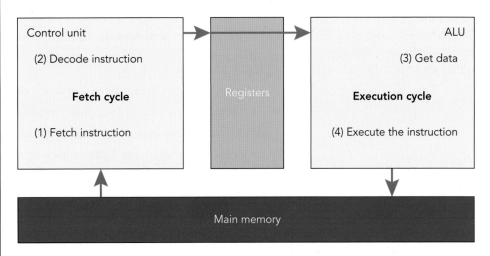

A diagrammatic summary of the fetch–decode–execute cycle.

Printing text is simple

When we start to program we normally start with 'Hello World'. This looks easy, but let's explore what is happening to display this on a screen. First, we type 'Hello'; this consists of separate letters 'H', 'E', 'L', 'L' and 'O'. If we now convert this to ASCII:

- H = Write 48 (hex)
- e = Write 65 (hex)
- l = Write 6C (hex)
- l = Write 6C (hex)
- o = Write 6F (hex).

We are now ready to write a machine-language program to implement the algorithm. There are six instructions in this program: five to write a character and one to indicate the end of the process.

The instruction to write a character on the screen is 11100, called the character output from operand operation. Should we store the characters in memory and write them using direct addressing or just store them in the operand specifier and use immediate addressing?

There are six instructions in our program. Remember the fetch–execute cycle? If the instructions are contiguous in memory, the process will start by loading 0000 into the counter. The instruction is decoded as a write character to output. This needs to be repeated for each character. So it's not such a simple process!

Mobile CPU and processors

Mobile devices are not connected to a power socket all the time so they need a long battery life. They are also small so do not have the space for fans to keep the CPU cool, which makes them prone to overheating. These design considerations are the reasons for the major differences between desktop and mobile CPUs. But the way the systems work is not so dissimilar.

What are the main differences between desktop and mobile CPUs?

■ The processor clock speed. The cooling requirements of any portable device require a processor that does not create too much heat. Portable processors always have lower clock speeds than their desktop equivalents as this reduces the amount of heat that they produce.

■ Space in a portable device is at a premium so most modern mobile processors also have other components integrated into the processor itself. These components often include things like wireless networking.

■ Mobile processors are also optimised for low power consumption.

Most modern smartphones have a dedicated processor for GSM (global system for mobile communications) and another (potentially multi-core) general-purpose processor for the user interface and applications. This processor is known as the application processor (AP), not the CPU as in other computing devices.

The GSM processor is often referred to as the BP processor after its function as a baseband radio processor, meaning that it handles the wireless internet and Bluetooth links.

Originally, each processor had its own memory (**RAM** and flash), peripherals, clock speed, and so on, but the search for smaller, more compact systems has led to a single RAM and flash chip being divided by assigning portions of the RAM and flash to each of the two processors.

Question

What is a clock cycle and why is it important?

Key term

RAM (random access memory) is the main memory of a computer used to store data, applications and the operating system while it is in use. When the power is turned off, RAM loses its data.

Question

What are the main differences between the processors used in mobile devices and desktop computers?

Multi-core processors in smartphones and tablets

A core is simply a distinct processing unit within a CPU. Most desktop and laptop computers have multi-core processors, but what about mobiles?

At first, smartphones had a single core, which was more than sufficient to handle the applications available. But modern smartphones and tablets have CPU-intensive applications and users want to multi-task. Users, for example, might want to watch a video, listen to music and play a game all at the same time. It is hard to push the clock speed as this increases power consumption. As we have seen, this is not what we want as the battery will not last long enough.

With dual-core processors, one core can process the game, while another processes the music. In this way, none of the cores is pushed to the limit and the overall power consumption of the phone is less.

The potential drawback is that many mobile programs are still not optimised for using multiple cores.

Memory

We have considered the importance of memory in any computing device. Just as humans have different kinds of memory, such as memory associated with walking, talking or other motor skills and short- and long-term memories, there are a number of different types of memory within computer systems.

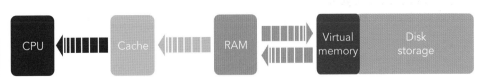

Memory in a computer system.

Using the diagram let's look at how this works. The CPU cannot fetch data directly from the hard disk. This is because even the slowest modern CPU processes data about 50 times faster than the fastest hard disk. We need fast memory and the fastest memory is our 'other' memory mentioned in the essential subcomponents of any system – **cache**.

Cache

Let's look at what the memory needs to store to make the computer work. The most important block of memory stores the software known as the operating system, then all the drivers for the input and output devices connected.

The cache is very high-speed memory and it draws data from memory called RAM as it is needed.

Question

What is meant by a dual-core processor?

Key term

Cache memory is special high-speed memory used by a computer.

RAM is much faster than the hard disk but even RAM is not fast enough for the CPU. You will see RAM described as 128- or 256-bit rate, but remember CPUs now often run at over 2 GHz. Computing devices need cache memory. But the problem is not only the speed of the memory device, but also how long it takes to fetch the data.

The cache's memory controllers have to predict which pieces of data the CPU will need next. They then collect it from the RAM and add it to their high-speed memory. This speeds up the system's performance. It is the operating system that has to control all of this. RAM can be supplemented by virtual memory but each step takes time and the hard disk is much slower than the RAM, which in turn is slower than the cache.

The data transfer between the operating system and all the input and output devices happens through the virtual nerves in the motherboard using a computer program called a driver. The driver has to translate electrical signals to and from the devices connected to the system so that the operating system and other programs can control them or receive data from them.

How does cache work?

To understand how cache works, let's start with an example. Imagine that you have lots of schoolbooks you need each week stored in desk drawers up in your bedroom. For this example let's say you are downstairs ready for school but you are too lazy to get the books yourself and you ask your mum or sister to go upstairs, find them and bring them to you. But then imagine how much quicker it would be if your mum or sister knew what books you would need and when you would need them. The books could then be kept close at hand downstairs, passing them to you as soon as you needed them, only putting them back with all the others in your drawers when they knew you would not need them for some time. This is how cache works. Of course, it cannot store all of your data; it has a limited size so it has a limit to how much it can store.

Cache technology uses very fast but small amounts of memory to speed up slower but larger memory types.

Cache memory is not only used inside your computer. It also helps in systems when data is transferred from very slow data sources, like the internet. Internet connections are the slowest links to your computer, so web browsers use their own cache on the web server to do the same task as your computer's cache, but for web pages. External hard drives also have their own cache memory.

Question

What is virtual memory and why is it needed?

Question

Describe the difference between ROM and RAM and how these are used in a computer.

New developments

We have looked at the clock speed of processors and explored how having a fast clock speed and a multi-core processor are of little value without cache, RAM and the programs to support it. This becomes even more complicated when we explore developments in mobile processors.

New designs allow CPUs to run at the same or at an even lower clock rate as older CPUs used in desktop computers, but which get more instructions completed per clock cycle. This makes it very difficult to use clock rates to compare processors made by different companies.

Smartphones and mobile devices such as tablet computers are equipped with more advanced embedded chipsets that can do far more tasks at the same time, providing they have been programmed correctly. The latest developments have seen engineers working on an integrated CPU and graphics processing unit (GPU).

You will probably come across references to level 1, 2 and even 3 cache. L1 is short for level 1 cache and this is always built into the CPU. L2 is short for level 2 cache, and this originally was external to the CPU on a separate microprocessor chip, but many modern processors now have this built in too. It is also sometimes called the secondary cache. As more and more CPUs begin to include L2 cache in their architectures, level 3 cache (L3) is the name given to the extra cache that is built into motherboards between the microprocessor and the main memory.

When the CPU finds data in the cache it is called a cache hit. References not found in the cache are called cache misses. When a cache miss occurs, the cache control mechanism must fetch the missing data from RAM and place it in the cache. The size and organisation of the cache are vitally important.

Cache organisation

There are three key principles involved in cache organisation:

- *Temporal locality.* When the CPU accesses a data source, the cache knows it is likely to need to access the same source again.
- *Spatial locality.* When the CPU accesses a particular location in memory, the cache knows that it is probable that it will also need to access data that is close to the original data.
- *Sequentiality locality.* When the CPU accesses a location s, it is likely that a reference to the location of $s + 1$ will also be needed.

Key points

An embedded system is a computer system, often on a chipset, that forms part of an electronic device.

Some devices contain what is called firmware. This is software that is stored permanently in a device, such as control programs for devices.

Questions

1 Why is locality important when dealing with cache?
2 Explain the purpose of level 2 cache (L2).

Cache size

There is no fixed cache size in CPUs, but the faster the CPU the larger the L2 cache needs to be. The size of the cache refers to the size of the data store. A typical L2 cache is 512 KB, but can be as high as 1 MB or even 2 MB. Within the CPU itself, level 1 (L1) cache is usually between 8 and 64 KB.

The more cache the system has, the more likely it is to register a hit when it accesses the RAM and so the faster it will operate.

Other types of cache

Away from the CPU we have cache for programs, the most common being web browser cache. Cache here serves the same purpose as in the CPU: it saves time when fetching frequently used data.

Whatever web browser you use to surf the internet, it will have a folder in which certain items that have been downloaded are stored for future access. Your browser assumes that you will want to view these again so it holds them in cache. Of course, it is not as sophisticated as the cache in a CPU and it only performs temporal locality as an organisation method.

The web browser cache stores images, photographs and even entire web pages. When you visit a page on a website, your computer first checks its cache folder to see if it already has any images displayed there and, if so, it won't take the time to download them again. This makes page loading faster, but can be a problem for web designers when they change items on a page and test the changes to only see the original page being drawn from the cache.

Cache folders can get very big and can occupy a large amount of hard drive space. It is advisable to empty the cache regularly and to limit the cache size.

Cache in programming

Once you understand the concepts of cache both to the CPU and to the way that computing systems work, you can use these concepts in your own programming for various applications and purposes.

In programming, a cache library can be used for storing database queries for later use. It can also be used to store rendered pages to save generating them again.

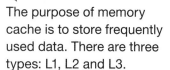

Key point

The purpose of memory cache is to store frequently used data. There are three types: L1, L2 and L3.

Random access memory (RAM)

You know that feeling when you are revising for tests and you feel that your brain is about to explode with too much information? Well, your computer would feel like that if it wasn't for the hard drive. When you are working on your computer, however, you only use a small amount of the information that is stored within it and because of this the computer transfers data from the hard drive to the random access memory (often abbreviated as RAM, or simply called memory). The cache memory is taken from the RAM when needed. If we go back to our schoolbook example, some of your most used books this week are taken from your desk drawer and stored at the top of the stairs.

A RAM module.

The advantage of using the RAM for storage of documents and so on, while you are working on them, is that RAM, although not as quick as cache, is fast, in fact much faster than any disk. What this means is that there is far less time waiting and more time being productive.

Like the CPU needs RAM to work efficiently, RAM is necessary on the graphics card as it has to keep the entire screen image in memory. When handling graphics, the CPU sends its data to the video card. The video processor forms a picture of the screen image and stores it in what is called the frame buffer. This picture is a large bitmap.

Some graphics cards use a special memory called VRAM (video RAM). A VRAM cell is made up of two ordinary RAM cells, which are fixed together. This double cell allows the processor to simultaneously read and write new data at the same RAM address.

Categories of memory

You might now be asking the questions: 'If RAM is so fast, why not put everything in it? In fact, why have a hard disk at all?' The answer to these questions is because RAM is volatile. What that means is that as soon

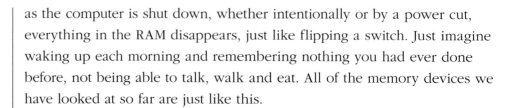

as the computer is shut down, whether intentionally or by a power cut, everything in the RAM disappears, just like flipping a switch. Just imagine waking up each morning and remembering nothing you had ever done before, not being able to talk, walk and eat. All of the memory devices we have looked at so far are just like this.

It would not be a useful idea to rely on RAM to hold everything. A hard disk drive, on the other hand, stores its information whether the power is on or off. Computing devices need somewhere safe to store data when they are switched off. For this they use either hard drives or flash memory.

We can now look at the two main categories of chip-based memory: volatile and non-volatile.

Volatile memory

Volatile memory is computer memory that requires a power supply in order to maintain stored data. In other words, volatile memory will store information as long as power is being supplied to it. The moment that power is turned off the information is lost. Volatile memory is often referred to as 'temporary memory'.

The RAM in your computer is a type of volatile memory. If there was a power cut when you were using your computer any unsaved documents that you were working on would be lost. This is the reason why you should get into the habit of frequently saving your work to the hard disk (which is non-volatile memory) while you work on your computer.

Normal RAM is dynamic (called DRAM). The advantage of the DRAM is that each stored data bit takes up a very small space. The disadvantage of this is that the stored charge doesn't last very long, so it has to be 'refreshed' periodically by a control circuit in the RAM stick. Static RAM has six transistors used to store each bit rather than the one on DRAM.

Several types of DRAM

There are several types of DRAM for computing devices and they are all quite different. This means that they cannot be used on the same motherboard as they are not compatible. Even when you find compatible DRAM for the same motherboard there will be different types, some more expensive than others.

You may have seen the word 'latency'. Latency is the time that it takes for the DRAM to respond. Imagine you are playing your favourite computer game and you are called for dinner. There will be a delay between your being called and your arrival to eat. This is latency. In DRAM, latency

Key term

Volatile memory cannot store data when the computing device is turned off. Non-volatile memory can.

Questions

1 Explain why some data is stored in RAM when you are running a program.
2 What kind of computer memory is both static and non-volatile?

is measured by the number of clicks of the system clock it takes for the DRAM to respond.

With volatile memory being solid state (that means it has no moving parts) it is able to process data far quicker than non-volatile memory such as hard disks. This is the reason why it is used for the DRAM within computers. We are talking about a latency of a single clock click of around 200 MHz. The latency of the DRAM needs to match the motherboard and CPU.

As we learned earlier, RAM is where programs that you wish to use are loaded up to from the hard disk. If you were to work with programs directly off the hard disk the latency would be much longer, and you would find the programs were sluggish and very slow to respond to your requests.

Key term

Buffering is a temporary storage area, usually but not always in RAM. The main purpose of buffers is to act as a holding area, enabling the computer to manipulate data before transferring it to a device.

Task

Explore the term print buffer.

Key term

ROM (read-only memory) is a store for data in a computer that cannot be overwritten. Data in ROM is always available and is not lost when the computer is turned off.

Question

What is the difference between DRAM and RAM?

Buffered DRAM

Most motherboards will hold four modules of DRAM but very high-performance computers will need more. To enable the motherboards to take more DRAM, special DRAM is needed. The DRAM modules have what are called **buffering** chips added. The term buffering is quite important in computing. In the case of DRAM the buffer controls the amount of electrical current that goes to and from the memory chips at any given time. This makes the DRAM more stable, but it also increases the cost of the DRAM modules and slows the RAM's speed.

Question

What type of memory is a USB drive and how does it work?

Non-volatile memory

Non-volatile memory is computer memory that will retain its information whether the power being supplied to it is turned on or off. Examples of non-volatile memory include **ROM** (read-only memory), flash memory, and most type of magnetic computer hard disks and optical disks. Interestingly, the early computer storage methods such as paper tape and punched cards are also referred to as non-volatile memory.

The purpose of non-volatile memory is for secondary or long-term persistent storage.

Question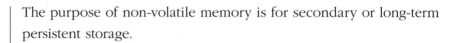

When your computer's speed begins to drop, explain which element of memory is likely to be almost full and describe how to improve the computer's memory performance.

Question

Explain a computer's memory hierarchy.

Key term

Virtual memory is a section of the hard disk used as if it were RAM to supplement the amount of main memory available to the computer.

Question

While a computer is working what is stored in RAM?

Virtual memory

The evolution of intelligent memory management procedures within computers has allowed an increase in the use of virtual memory. This is achieved by putting some sections of RAM on to the hard disk. Of course, latency times are extended but the RAM capacity is extended as well. The name for this type of RAM is **virtual memory**.

Why add virtual memory?

Let's say that your computer only has 1 GB of RAM and you attempt to run a few programs that require memory of around 1.5 GB. Without virtual memory, an error message would appear indicating that your memory was full. But with virtual memory, the operating system assigns a part of the hard disk as RAM and keeps the data there.

In our example let's assume that the virtual memory is also 1 GB: 1 GB actual memory + 1 GB virtual memory = 2 GB memory. So even though your RAM module is relatively small, you can still use memory-intensive applications.

Unfortunately, there is a disadvantage to using virtual memory. Reading data from a hard disk is much slower than reading from solid-state RAM and so the more information that is stored in your hard disk the slower your system becomes, making it appear sluggish.

Questions

1 How does virtual memory free up RAM?
2 Explain the term latency.

Data is stored on physical devices and this can include magnetic, optical and solid-state devices. The most important storage device is the hard disk drive.

Hard disk drive

The original iPod music player was not much more than a hard drive. Hard drives are efficient computer memory devices that use magnetism to store data.

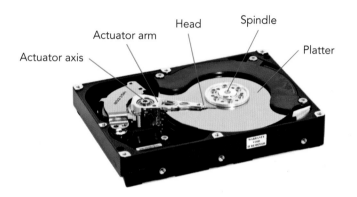

A hard disk drive with the top cover removed.

The CPU in your computer is the 'brain' that does all the thinking, but it's the hard drive that lets you store your data, music, photos, music files and text documents. It is also the hard drive that holds the programs.

The slowest type of memory is the hard drive, but it is the largest memory device in terms of the amount of data it can hold. All of the information that is stored within your computer is stored on its hard disk drive. When you switch on your device it is the hard disk that first sends the operating data to the RAM, cache and CPU.

You never see that actual hard disk because it is sealed inside a special housing within the case of the computer or device. In a similar way to your long-term memory, the hard disk can hold information almost forever – with or without electricity.

Most modern hard disks can have billions of bytes of storage space on them, which means that you can create, save and download files for months or years without fear of using up all the drive's storage space. If you do manage to fill up your hard disk, your operating system will start informing you by way of a message on your screen saying something like: 'You are running low on disk space.' Don't worry, this will happen well in advance of any storage problems occurring.

Solid-state hard drives are really large flash memory disks. Because they have no moving parts they are much faster, smaller and more robust than traditional hard drives.

Read-only memory (ROM)

We found out that RAM 'forgets' what it knows when the computer's power is switched off. There is another type of memory called read-only memory (ROM) that does not forget when the power is switched off.

ROM chips have data preinstalled on them during manufacture. The information is stored on them permanently and cannot be changed. This makes them excellent for small mobile devices, where they hold the operating system.

Flash memory

Small portable devices such as MP3 players, phones and cameras need small portable memory. They use special chips called **flash memory** to store information permanently. Flash memory has certain things in common with both ROM and RAM as it remembers information when the power is off but it can also be erased and rewritten many times. You also find flash memory in memory sticks.

Task

Investigate the sizes of flash memory drives available and their cost per GB of capacity.

Flash memory does not use magnetism like hard disk drives; it uses a transistor that stays switched on (or switched off) when the power is turned off. Remember that computers remember everything in binary, so this system works well with all computing needs.

Is it better to have more memory or a faster processor?

This is often the biggest question manufacturers and computer buyers have to consider, particularly with regard to RAM. As we have seen in earlier chapters, whenever the computer is manipulating information it is placed in the memory to be retrieved or manipulated later. Each block of memory, used or not, is allocated by the program.

Once all the usable memory has been filled up, the computer has to store temporary data on the hard drive in a space referred to as a swap file. Once data is in a swap file the CPU has to undertake a two-step process to first write then read the data, rather than a single-step process of reading the data from faster memory.

Question

In the world of computing, what is bus width?

Key term

Flash memory is solid-state memory used as secondary storage in portable devices and is also used as removable memory in things like USB drives.

Key point

Solid state refers to technology that is based on electronics with no moving parts, for example transistors and capacitors when used in memory chips.

Question

What is the brain of the computer called?

If we add to this the speed difference between the very fast RAM and the comparatively slow hard drive, you can see how extra memory of the right type of RAM can be just as useful as a faster CPU.

Graphics cards (GPU)

When using programs such as computer games or 3D images, the graphics card is just as important as a good screen. The graphics card supports the CPU. It has a processor like the CPU. However, it is especially designed to control screen images. Imagine having a friend who is very good at drawing. When you need to illustrate something, rather than do it yourself, you ask your friend to do it for you. This is how a graphics card works: it helps out the CPU whenever graphics are needed. It does nothing else, but this can be a very hard task.

Remember that the images you see on your screen are made of thousands of tiny dots called pixels. Most screens display well over a million pixels, and the computer has to decide what to do with each and every one in order to create the image that you see on the monitor. It is the job of the graphics card to translate all the ones and zeros into pictures and words.

To make a 3D image, the graphics card has to work even harder. First, it creates a wire-frame image using straight lines, then it fills in the frame with pixels. The name given to this is rendering. Then it adds texture, colour and lighting effects. And it has to do all this over 60 times a second during a video game.

The graphics card can be a separate circuit that slots into the computer. The advantage of this type of card is that it can be upgraded.

The graphics card in laptops and handheld devices is an integral part of the system's motherboard and cannot be changed.

A graphics card consists of two components:
- A video chip set, which creates the signals that the screen must receive to form an image.
- RAM, which is necessary since the video card must be able to remember a complete screen image at any time.

Optical drives

Optical drives retrieve and/or store data on optical disks such as CDs, DVDs and BDs (Blu-ray disks). Burning data to CDs and DVDs is the most common method of copying and backing up data at home and you have probably done it yourself.

Question

Why does a computer have both RAM and cache memory?

Data is burned on to the surface of a disk using a laser beam contained within the drive. The laser is also used to read the data from the disk.

The typical storage capacity of a CD is 650 MB of data, whereas a single-sided DVD can store up to 4.7 GB of data. A double-sided DVD can store 9 GB.

CDs and DVDs use a red laser to read and write data. Blu-ray disks use a blue–violet laser, which is why they are called Blu-ray. Blu-ray disks hold 25–50 GB of data and some new types can store 500 GB on a single disk by using 20 layers.

There are basically two types of optical media:

- CD-ROM, DVD-R and BR-R, where the 'R' indicates that the media is read-only memory, meaning that data can only be written once and after that occasion the disk cannot be written to again. It can, however, be read and replayed endless times.
- CD-RW, DVD-RW and BR-RW, where the 'RW' indicates that the media is rewritable, meaning that you can save data to the disk repeatedly.

One problem with optical media is that the different companies that manufacture them have not agreed on a standard format. Because of this you will see numerous types of DVD such as DVD-R, DVD+R, DVD-RW and DVD+RW. You should always make sure you buy the correct type of optical media for your computer's drive.

Computer hardware: peripherals

We have talked about the hardware that forms the system unit, but as you are probably aware there are many devices that exist outside the computer that are referred to as hardware. Basically, every hardware device that is outside the system unit is referred to as a peripheral. Even though peripheral devices do not form part of the core system unit they are often, but not always, partially or completely dependent on the host computer.

Understanding input and output devices is essential to a programmer. But almost all modern computing peripherals require both input and output to do anything useful. Even a sheet of paper has input to record ideas and output to display the ideas.

A mouse in computing terms is an input device, yet often has a click when the button is pressed (output) and a cursor movement on the screen (output).

Task

Identify the various input and output devices typically found on a tablet computer and describe their purpose.

Input and output are becoming even more blurred with advanced computer interfaces such as mobile devices and gaming consoles. The role of inputs and outputs is to link our human minds and actions with the computer processor.

One of the main issues with input devices is that they often influence the user's ability to input data. Etch A Sketch, for example, is easier to use when drawing a square than a circle. Hence the choice of device influences the level of skill required.

Traditional peripherals can be categorised into three different groups: *input*, *output* and *storage*. Input devices provide data into the computer and include:

- barcode readers
- graphics tablets
- image scanners
- joysticks
- keyboards

- mice
- microphones
- touchscreens
- webcams.

Output devices display or present processed data to the user from the computer and include:

- headphones
- monitors
- plotters
- printers
- speakers.

Some devices are both input and output devices:

- headphones
- read–write optical drives
- touchscreens
- USB drives.

Storage peripherals are also usually input/output devices. They are used to store data in between work sessions on the computer and include devices such as:

- external hard drives
- flash drives
- smartphones or tablet computers.

Let's take a closer look at some of these peripheral devices.

Question

Typically, what technology do hard disk drives employ as a storage mechanism?

Secondary storage devices

The majority of secondary storage devices are used to:

- add more storage space for files, pictures, videos and so on
- back up data
- easily transport files
- share files over a network
- transfer files between computers.

Non-volatile secondary storage

Different types of non-volatile **secondary storage** include:

- flash memory cards
- magnetic storage
- optical storage: compact disk (CD), digital versatile disk (DVD) and Blu-ray disk (BD)
- solid-state disks
- USB drives.

Magnetic storage devices

A **magnetic hard disk** drive uses moving read/write heads that contain electromagnets. These create a magnetic charge on the disk's surface which contains iron particles that can be given a magnetic charge in one of two directions. Each magnetic particle's direction represents 0 (off) or 1 (on). As you will remember, these represent a bit of data that the CPU can recognise.

The advantages of hard disk drives include the following:

- Data is not lost when you switch off the computer, as it is with RAM.
- They are cheap per gigabyte compared to other storage media.
- They can easily be replaced and upgraded.
- They have very large data storage capacity.
- They store and retrieve data much faster than optical disks.

The disadvantages of hard disk drives include the following:

- Crashes can damage the surface of the disk, leading to a loss of data.
- Hard disks have moving parts which eventually fail.
- They are easily damaged if dropped.
- They can be noisy.
- They use a large amount of power compared to other media.

Optical storage devices

An **optical drive** uses reflected light to read data. The optical disk's surface is covered with tiny dents (pits) and flat spots (lands), which cause laser light to be reflected off them differently. When an optical drive shines light into a pit, the light is not reflected back. This represents a bit value of 0 (off). When the light shines on a flat surface (land) it reflects light back to the sensor, representing a bit value of 1 (on).

The advantages of optical drives include the following:
■ Optical disks are read in a number of devices such as audio and television systems.
■ They are easy to store and carry.
■ They are long lasting if looked after properly.
■ They are very easy to use.

The disadvantages of optical drives include the following:
■ Data on write-once disks (CD, DVD and BD) is permanent and cannot be changed.
■ Optical disks require special drives to read and write.
■ Optical storage is expensive per gigabyte in comparison to other methods.
■ There are no standards for longevity tests.
■ They can easily be broken.
■ They can easily be scratched and damaged by heat and light.

Solid-state disks

Solid-state disks contain no moving parts. They record data using special transistors that retain their state even when there is no power to them. Because there is no moving actuator arm like on a hard disk drive they are faster in reading and, in some cases, writing data. They are also more rugged so are not as easily damaged when dropped.

The advantages of solid-state disks include the following:
■ Their read speeds are faster than normal hard disk drives.
■ They are free from mechanical problems.
■ They are lightweight.
■ They are silent in use.
■ They are very durable.
■ They have non-volatile memory, which means that data is stable.
■ They require less power than magnetic drives.

The disadvantages of solid-state disks include the following:
■ Information can only be erased and written about 100000 times.
■ Random write speeds of solid-state drives can be four times slower than normal magnetic hard disk drives.
■ The cost per gigabyte stored is higher than magnetic drives.

Question

Why is there a limited number of tracks on an audio CD?

■ They have limited storage capacity when compared to normal magnetic hard disk drives.

Memory sticks/USB drives

USB flash drives use the same technology as solid-state drives. They are a more compact shape and operate faster than an external magnetic drive due to their lack of moving parts. Flash drives are widely used to transport files and back up data from computer to computer.

The advantages of flash drives include the following:
■ Adding or deleting files in flash memory is quick and easy.
■ They are free from mechanical problems.
■ They are lightweight.
■ They are silent in use.
■ They are small and easily portable.
■ They are very durable.
■ They do not need an internal power supply.
■ They have non-volatile memory, which means that data is stable.
■ They require less power than magnetic drives.

The disadvantages of flash drives include the following:
■ Information can only be erased and written about 100 000 times.
■ The cost per gigabyte stored is higher than magnetic drives.
■ They can be affected by electronic corruption and this can make the data totally unreadable.
■ They can be lost or misplaced.
■ They can break easily.

Flash memory cards

A memory card or flash memory card also uses a solid-state drive using flash memory. They are often used with digital cameras, handheld computers, mobile telephones, music players, video game consoles and other types of small electronic devices.

The advantages of flash memory cards include the following:
■ Adding or deleting files in flash memory is quick and easy.
■ Memory cards have non-volatile memory, which means that data is stable.
■ They are free from mechanical problems.
■ They are lightweight.
■ They are silent in use.
■ They are small and easily portable.
■ They are very durable.

Task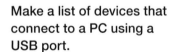

Make a list of devices that connect to a PC using a USB port.

■ They do not need internal power.

■ They require less power than magnetic drives.

The disadvantages of flash memory cards include the following:

■ Information can only be erased and written about 100 000 times.

■ There are many different formats and sizes, making them often only suited to one device and hard to read across devices.

■ They can be affected by electronic corruption and this can make the data totally unreadable.

■ They can be lost or misplaced.

■ They can break easily.

■ The cost per gigabyte stored is higher than magnetic drives.

Microcontrollers

Microcontrollers can be programmed to control devices. Microcontrollers are hidden inside a large number of everyday objects. If your microwave oven has a screen and a keypad, it probably contains a microcontroller.

All modern cars contain at least one microcontroller, and some cars have more than one. Most modern engines are controlled by microcontrollers, The brakes and the cruise control also have microcontrollers.

All of your electronic equipment that uses remote controls will have a microcontroller. This includes televisions and stereo systems. Digital cameras, mobile phones, camcorders, laser printers, telephones and even the latest refrigerators, dishwashers, washers and dryers have them. Basically, any product or device designed to interact with a user will contain a microcontroller.

What is a microcontroller?

Microcontrollers are basically small computers. Like all computers they have:

■ a CPU that executes programs

■ some RAM where they can store 'variables'

■ some input and output devices.

Desktop and laptop computers can be referred to as 'general-purpose computers' as they can run many different programs. In contrast to this, microcontrollers would be called 'special-purpose computers' as they do one thing well.

Microcontrollers have a number of other distinctive characteristics:

■ They are usually **embedded** in other devices. They are used to control the features or actions of the other device.

Question

Describe the benefits and drawbacks of using a traditional magnetic hard disk drive in a laptop computer compared to a solid-state hard drive.

Key term

Embedded systems usually form part of an electronic device. They are the lowest level of an operating system that controls the hardware.

- They are dedicated to one task and run one specific program. The program does not change and is stored in ROM.
- They are usually low-power devices. A battery-operated microcontroller usually consume less than 60 milliwatts.
- A microcontroller takes input from the device it is controlling and controls the device by sending signals to different components in the device.

Programming microcontrollers

Microcontrollers are usually programmed using what is called a basic stamp. You program a basic stamp using the BASIC programming language. Standard BASIC instructions include:

- *for ... next* (the normal looping statement)
- *go sub* (go to a subroutine)
- *goto* (go to a label in the program)
- *if ... then* (the normal if–then decision statement)
- *end* (end the program and sleep).

BASIC logic statements include:

- =
- <>
- <
- <=

- >
- >=
- AND
- OR.

Raspberry Pi

A Raspberry Pi computer.

The Raspberry Pi is a microcontroller you may have come across. It is only the size of a credit card but it is a fully functioning single-board computer. It was developed in the UK by the Raspberry Pi Foundation to help promote the teaching of computer science in schools.

Actuators and sensors

Microprocessors use actuators and sensors to function.

Actuators

An actuator is used to move or control output. It is a type of motor for moving or controlling a mechanism or system. To operate, it needs a source of energy, usually in the form of electric current, hydraulic fluid pressure or pneumatic pressure. The actuator converts that energy into motion.

Sensors

A sensor is a converter that measures a physical quantity and converts it into a signal. The microcontroller uses this signal to make a decision based on its stamp. For example, a thermometer converts the measured temperature into expansion and contraction of a liquid, which indicates the temperature on markings on the thermometer's casing. Of course, this is not digital but analogue, and microcontrollers need digital signals. In microcontrollers, a thermocouple converts temperature to an output voltage which can then be read.

A sensor is therefore a device which responds to an input quantity by generating a digital output in the form of an electrical or optical signal.

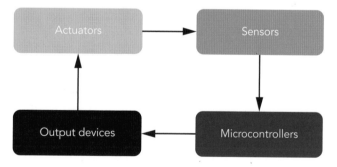

A summary of actuators and sensors.

Sensors in everyday objects

Modern smartphones have a wide variety of sensors that automate or make easy many of our daily tasks.

- *Accelerometer.* An accelerometer measures linear acceleration of movement. An accelerometer sensor will measure the directional movement of a device but cannot measure lateral orientation or tilt; for this a gyroscope sensor is needed.

- *Barometer.* A barometer sensor measures altitude. The barometer is there to help the phone's global positioning system (GPS) chip lock on to GPS signals by delivering altitude data.
- *Digital compass.* The digital compass sensor in a phone is usually based on a sensor called a magnetometer. This sensor provides smartphones with a simple orientation in relation to the Earth's magnetic field. In this way, the phone always knows which way is north and can autorotate digital maps.
- *Gyroscope.* Gyroscope (gyro) sensors are used to detect the orientation of a device. A gyro sensor measures the angular rotational velocity. As such, the sensor tracks a phone's rotation or twist.

16 Logic

Learning outcomes

- Be able to construct truth tables for a given logic statement.
- Be able to produce logic statements for a given problem.

Logic statements

Any given electronic signal has a level of voltage. We distinguish between the two values of interest (binary 0 and 1) by the voltage level of a signal. A voltage level in the range of 0–2 volts is considered low and is interpreted as a binary 0. A voltage level in the range of 2–5 volts is considered high and is interpreted as a binary 1.

Signals in a computer are constrained to be within one range or the other. A gate is a device that performs a basic operation on electrical signals. A gate accepts one or more input signals and produces a single output signal.

There are several specific types of gate. Each type of gate performs a particular logical function. Gates are combined into circuits to perform more complicated tasks. These gates in a computer are sometimes referred to as logic gates because they each perform one logical function. Each gate accepts one or more input values and produces a single output value.

Here is a list of the six most popular logic gates:

- NOT
- AND
- OR
- XOR
- NAND
- NOR.

NOT gate

A NOT gate accepts one input value and produces one output value.

The diagram shows a NOT gate represented in three ways: as a Boolean expression, as its logical diagram symbol and using a **truth table**. In each representation, the variable A represents the input signal, which is either 0 or 1. The variable X represents the output signal, whose value (also 0 or 1) is determined by the value of A.

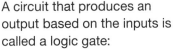

Key point

A circuit that produces an output based on the inputs is called a logic gate:

NOT: a logic gate that outputs the opposite value to the input

AND: a logic gate that outputs 1 if both inputs are 1

OR: a logic gate that outputs 1 if either, or both, of the two inputs are 1.

Key term

A **truth table** is a method for recording all the possible input combinations and determining the output for each when using logic gates.

Boolean expression	Logic diagram symbol	Truth table

$X = \backslash"$

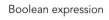

A	X
0	1
1	0

The NOT gate represented as a Boolean expression, a logic diagram symbol and a truth table.

A NOT gate is sometimes referred to as an inverter because it inverts the input value. The truth table in the diagram shows all possible input values for a NOT gate, as well as the corresponding output values.

Keep in mind that these three notations are just different ways of representing the same thing.

AND gate

An AND gate is shown in the diagram. Note how an AND gate accepts two input signals. The values of both input signals determine what the output signal will be. If the two input values for an AND gate are both 1, the output is 1; otherwise, the output is 0.

Boolean expression	Logic diagram symbol	Truth table

$X = \backslash - e$

 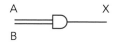

A	B	X
0	0	0
0	1	0
1	0	0
1	1	1

The AND gate represented as a Boolean expression, a logic diagram symbol and a truth table.

Key point

Boolean algebra is a method for expressing a logic circuit mathematically.

There are four possible situations that can occur using the AND operator in a Boolean expression:

- 0 0 equals 0
- 0 1 equals 0
- 1 0 equals 0
- 1 1 equals 1.

OR gate

An OR gate is shown in the diagram. It also has two inputs. If the two input values are both 0, the output value is 0; otherwise, the output is 1.

	Boolean expression	Logic diagram symbol		Truth table	

X = \ 1 e

A	B	X
0	0	0
0	1	1
1	0	1
1	1	1

The **OR** gate represented as a Boolean expression, a logic diagram symbol and a truth table.

XOR gate

The XOR, or exclusive OR, gate is shown in the diagram.

Boolean expression   Logic diagram symbol   Truth table

X = \ ⊕ e

A	B	X
0	0	0
0	1	1
1	0	1
1	1	0

The **XOR** gate represented as a Boolean expression, a logic diagram symbol and a truth table.

An XOR gate produces 0 if its two inputs are the same, and a 1 otherwise.

NAND and NOR gates

The NAND and NOR gates are shown in the diagrams.

Boolean expression   Logic diagram symbol   Truth table

X = o\ – eE"

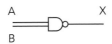

A	B	X
0	0	1
0	1	1
1	0	1
1	1	0

The **NAND** gate represented as a Boolean expression, a logic diagram symbol and a truth table.

Boolean expression   Logic diagram symbol   Truth table

X = o\ 1 eE"

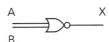

A	B	X
0	0	1
0	1	0
1	0	0
1	1	0

The **NOR** gate represented as a Boolean expression, a logic diagram symbol and a truth table.

The NAND and NOR gates are the opposite of the AND and OR gates, respectively. That is, the output of a NAND gate is the same as if you took the output of an AND gate and put it through an inverter (a NOT gate).

Gates with more inputs

Gates can be designed to accept three or more input values. A three-input AND gate, for example, produces an output of 1 only if all input values are 1.

Boolean expression	Logic diagram symbol	Truth table

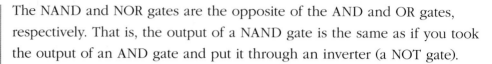

A	B	C	X
0	0	0	0
0	0	1	0
0	1	0	0
0	1	1	0
1	0	0	0
1	0	1	0
1	1	0	0
1	1	1	1

The three-input OR gate represented as a Boolean expression, a logic diagram symbol and a truth table.

17 Software

Software infrastructures

So far we have looked at code and the hardware that makes up a computing device. We have even looked at how code is written, but computing devices need to have both hardware and software infrastructures to function. In this chapter we will explore some of the software infrastructures.

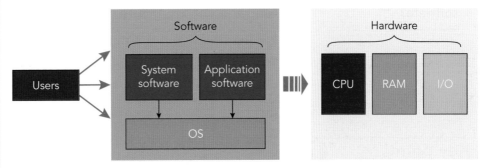

A diagrammatic representation of a computing device.

Operating system

The operating system (often just called the OS) is at the very heart of the computer. The OS is basically a collection of software that manages computer hardware resources and provides services for computer programs.

Some of the most popular operating systems are listed below:

- AIX
- Android phone
- Blackberry (RIM OS)
- iOS (iPhoneOS)
- IOS (Cisco)
- IronWare OS (Foundry)
- Linux
- Macintosh OS X (Mac OS X)
- Solaris (SunOS)

Question

State three examples of operating systems which are used in different computer devices.

- Windows
- Windows CE
- XOS (Extreme Networks).

Here are just a few of the tasks that operating systems carry out:

- control over system performance
- co-ordination between other software and users
- device management
- error detecting
- file management
- memory management
- processor management
- security.

You can see just how important the OS is.

The main tasks of the OS can be summarised into three main functions.

Manage the computer resources

For the OS to do this it must manage the CPU, allocation of memory, access to disk drives, control of printers and much more. All the input–output functions of the computer are controlled by the OS.

Question

What is operating system software?

Interact with the user

Users must have some means of interacting with a computer for it to be of any use. The OS provides the means of doing this, ideally in an easy, consistent, flexible and structured manner.

Run applications

The application packages that a user needs such as word processors and spreadsheets are what most people use a computer for. Without an OS these packages could not execute (run). The OS also provides these applications with tools and services such as printing and fetching data from a hard disk.

With graphical operating systems, the application also manages the menu facilities and windows supported by and provided with the OS.

Key point

There are two types of system software: operating system and utility programs.

Abstraction

We have looked at this word before as it is very important in computer science, but it is worth revisiting. In simple terms, the idea of abstracting is like hiding or ignoring details that are unimportant in any context. You are reading this book. You are not thinking about each of the individual letters or how they have been made with blobs of ink. You are seeing words and sentences. In a similar way, an OS hides away certain details that are not needed at any particular time. An example from real life is money. Originally, everyone had to barter or, say, swap a cow for the eight chickens they wanted. It was hard if you could not find someone with what you wanted who would exchange it for what you had to offer. Money came about because it provided a common way to exchange things with other people. You pay money for what you want and the seller doesn't care about what you sold to get the money. Money is therefore a good example of an abstraction.

Operating systems provide a common way to access a variety of hardware when it is needed. They offer another level of abstraction.

You may be asking a question: if an OS is trying to keep programs from having to worry about hardware differences, why are there different operating systems? Each OS was developed by different companies to suit different hardware systems. It is like all the world's countries having money but using different currencies. Most currencies can be exchanged for one another. In a similar way, virtual machines can run another OS inside a parent OS. It is just yet another level of abstraction.

Application software

Key term

Application software consists of programs that perform specific tasks.

Application software is computer software that causes a computer to perform useful tasks beyond the running of the computer itself. Such software is often called a software application, a program, an application or an app.

The word application is used because each program has a specific application for the user. For example, a word processor can help a user to write a document.

Applications are programs designed to run under an OS. They are a further abstraction from the hardware. They range from word processors and web browsers to video games and media players. Examples of application software include:
- 3D computer graphics software
- animation software
- data manipulation (databases and spreadsheets)
- digital audio editor
- graphic art software
- image editing software
- image organisers
- media content creating/editing

- music sequencer
- sound editing software
- text editors (word processors, desk-top publishing)
- vector graphics editor
- video editing software.

Web browsers, email programs, word processors, games and utilities are all software applications.

Macintosh programs were always called applications, but Windows programs were referred to as executable files. This is why Mac programs use the .APP file extension and Windows use the .EXE extension. But whatever the extension, both Macintosh and Windows programs serve the same purpose, so both should be called software applications.

Modelling

You have already done some modelling in this book because flowcharts and pseudocode are methods of modelling computer programs. They are both abstractions. But computer software has an amazing capacity to model things in the real world and to ask 'what if?' questions about all manner of things.

A model can come in many shapes, sizes and styles. A model is not the real world, it is merely a human construct to help us better understand the real world and its systems. All models have an information input, an information processing stage and an output of results.

Models usually start off as conceptual models. These help to highlight important connections in real-world systems and processes.

Mathematical and statistical models have been used since the first computers. They involve solving relevant equation(s) of a system. The system is usually based on its statistical parameters such as mean, mode, variance or regression coefficients. Mathematical models are useful in helping to identify patterns and underlying relationships between data sets. You will have probably come across spreadsheet modelling, which is one type of software model. You will know that the model needs some sort of data and a set of rules to manipulate the data and arrive at an outcome.

Many of the most recent models use visualisation. Visualisation links the data to some sort of graphic or image output. Using this type of software model it is possible to predict weather patterns such as the possible route of a storm.

Question

What is a supercomputer and what is it used for?

18 Programming languages

Learning outcomes

- Understand what is meant by high-level and low-level programming languages and assess their suitability for a particular task.
- Understand what is meant by a compiler and an interpreter.

High- and low-level programming languages

In computer science, a low-level programming language is a programming language that provides little or no abstraction from a computer's instruction set **architecture**. As we have already covered, abstraction is the process of extracting the underlying essence of a concept, removing any dependence on the real code needed. It refers to the distinction between the properties of an entity and its internal needs. It is abstraction that allows us to ignore the internal details of a complex device such as a computer, car or microwave oven and just use it.

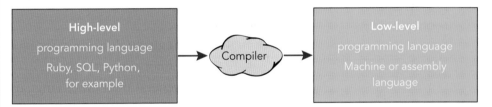

The relationship between high- and low-level programming languages.

Assembly language is at the level of telling the processor what to do – you cannot get much more low level than that. The 'low' refers to the small or non-existent amount of abstraction between the language used and machine language. Because of this, low-level languages are often described as being 'close to the hardware'. The code is what the hardware uses.

A low-level language does not need a compiler or an interpreter to run. The processor for which the language was written is able to run the code without using these to translate the code into something they understand.

The programming language C is a step higher up from assembler language because you get to specify what you want to do in more abstract terms. You're still fairly close though to the low-level language needed. C++ does everything that C can do but adds the capability to abstract things into classes.

Java and C# do similar things to C++, but without the opportunity to do everything you can do in C (like pointer manipulation in Java's case).

By comparison, a high-level programming language isolates the actual language needed by the machine from the code written, making the process of developing a program simpler and more understandable to the average human.

Python and Ruby are higher level as they let the programmer forget about many of the details that they would need to specify in something like Java or C#.

SQL is even higher level (it's declarative). The programmer just says 'give me all the items in the table sorted by age' and SQL will work out the most efficient and best way to carry this instruction out.

Let's now consider some high- and low-level programming languages and their advantages and disadvantages.

Python

Advantages

- A high-level language. It is good for rapid prototyping and applications where speed is not supercritical.
- A little more general than other languages, in that it does pretty much everything: web, standalone GUI, graphics, mobile, quick scripts and so on.
- Code has to be strictly indented but the indentation helps the code in being easy to read.
- Does not enforce a strict type on containers or variables.
- Does not use any syntax, instead tabbing and spacing play an important role in program flow.
- Easier to learn than Java or C.
- Easy to write, easy to read and easy to understand.
- Programs are three to five times smaller than Java programs.
- Program length is five to 10 times shorter than in C++.
- The integration of Python with languages such as Java and C/C++ allows Python to remove some stress from the interpreter.
- Very robust because of its lack of syntax. Users with little to no experience of Python can quickly determine program functionality and begin refactoring code for upgrades or bug fixes.
- With the absence of syntax, developers wishing to use Python need not learn any new rules.

Question

Describe the differences between a high-level language and an assembly language.

Disadvantages

- Adds the overhead on interpretation to the runtime of the program which can lead to a slower runtime. It is estimated that Python runs one to five times slower then Java or C/C++.
- Because of its lack of syntax, Python is an easy language to program in. However, it is not very simple to translate a Python program into any other language.
- Doesn't really do multi-processor or multi-core work very well.
- Programs run slower than Java codes.
- Python is an 'interpreted language' and C++ is a 'compiled language'. Because of this Python code is slower than C++ code.

Java

Advantages

- Can run on any computer.
- Can run on most smartphones.
- It is distributed and involves several computers on a network working together.
- It is object oriented, because programming in Java is centred on creating objects, manipulating objects and making objects work together. This allows programmers to create modular programs and reusable code.
- Multi-threaded: it can perform several tasks simultaneously within a program.
- One of the first programming languages to consider security as part of its design. The Java language, compiler, interpreter and runtime environment were each developed with security in mind.
- Simple: Java was designed to be easy to use and is therefore easy to write, compile, debug and learn compared to other programming languages.
- Uses automatic memory allocation and garbage collection.
- Very robust. Robust means reliable, although no programming language can really ensure reliability.

Disadvantages

- A much more complicated language than C.
- An interpreter is needed in order to run Java programs. The programs are compiled into Java virtual machine code called bytecode.
- Can be perceived as significantly slower and more memory consuming than natively compiled languages such as C or C++.
- Slow, not only slow to run, but also slow to develop.
- Works best as a high-level enterprise web application.

C++

Advantages

- A good language for engineers.
- A good language with which to write operating systems, drivers and platform-dependent applications. A good language to use to learn how to program.
- Best suited for general-purpose and low-level programming.
- Extremely fast, works very well for GUI programming on a computer.

Disadvantages

- Although it is platform independent, it is mostly used for platform-specific applications.
- Difficult to debug when used for web applications.
- Overly complex for very large high-level programs.

C#

Advantages

- Can be used for web applications on Microsoft computers.
- Works well with the Microsoft product line.

Disadvantage

- Almost completely locks you into the Microsoft platform.

Compilers and interpreters

As you will know by now, computers can only understand machine-level language (binary: zeros and ones).

It is difficult to write and maintain programs in high-level machine language. The programs written in the code of high- and low-level languages need to be converted into machine-level language using **translators** for this purpose. Only assembly language does not need any real conversion from abstraction. Each step from low- to high-level language is another level of abstraction.

Translators are just computer programs that accept a program written in high- or low-level languages and produce an equivalent machine-level program as an output. These translators are of one of three types:

- assembler
- compiler
- interpreter.

Key point

Binary is a system of numbers using only two digits, 0 and 1 (also called the base-2 system), unlike the decimal (or denary) system in everyday use that uses 1 to 10 (base-10).

Key term

A translator is a program to convert high-level or assembly-level commands into machine code.

An assembler is used to assemble the code of a low-level language into machine-level language. An assembler translates each instruction in the source program into a single machine instruction.

Compilers and interpreters are used to convert the code of high-level languages into machine language. The high-level program is known as a source program and the corresponding machine-level program is known as an object program.

Although both compilers and interpreters perform essentially the same task, there is a difference in the way they work. A compiler searches all the errors of a program and lists them. If the program is error free then it converts the code of the program into **machine code**.

An interpreter checks the errors of a program statement by statement. After checking one statement, it converts that statement into machine code and then executes that statement. The process continues until the last statement of program occurs. Rather than producing a machine-language copy of a program that will be executed later, an interpreter actually executes a program from its high-level form.

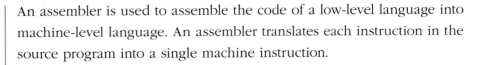

Question

What is a low-level programming language?

Key term

Machine code is the instruction in binary used by the CPU.

Task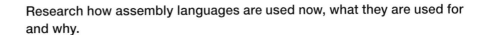

Research how assembly languages are used now, what they are used for and why.

Topic 5
COMMUNICATION AND THE INTERNET

19 Networks and the world wide web

Learning outcomes

- Understand why computers are connected in a network.
- Understand the different types of networks.
- Understand the network media.
- Understand that network data speeds are measured in bits per second.
- Understand the role of and the need for network protocols.
- Understand that data can be transmitted over networks using packets.
- Understand the need to detect and correct errors in data transmission.
- Understand the concept of and need for network addressing and host names.
- Understand the characteristics of network topologies.
- Understand what is meant by the internet and how the internet is structured.
- Understand what is meant by the world wide web (WWW) and components of the WWW.
- Be able to use HTML and CSS to construct web pages.
- Understand the client–server model, the difference between client-side and server-side processing and the role of cookies.

Definition of a computer network

A computer network can be described as two or more computers connected through a communication media. The purpose of a computer network is to exchange information and data, and networked computers can use the resources of other computers.

There are a number of basic components of computer networks and these are described below.

- *Servers*. A **server** is generally a powerful computer that provides services to the other computers on the network.
- *Clients*. A **client** is a computer that uses the services that a server provides. Clients are generally less powerful than the server within a network.
- *Communication media*. The physical connection between the devices on a network. This could be through a cable in an organisation's local network, a wireless signal or the internet. Network data speeds are measured in the number of bits per second: either megabits per second (Mbps) or gigabits per second (Gbps).
- *Network adapter*. Often referred to as the network interface card (NIC), this is a circuit board that is equipped with the components necessary for sending and receiving data. It is usually plugged into one of the available slots on a computer and a transmission cable is attached to the connector on the NIC.

Key terms

A **server** provides services to a client.

The **client** requests services from a server.

- *Resources.* Any peripheral device that is available to a client on the network such as printers, fax devices and other network devices. However, the word also refers to data and information.
- *User.* Any person who uses a client to access resources on a network.
- *Protocols.* The protocols of a network are formal, written rules used for the network communications. They are essentially the languages that computers use to communicate between each other on a network.

Advantages and disadvantages of computer networks

There are a number of advantages to using networks, which include:

- A network allows users to share software stored in a main system.
- Files can easily be shared between users over a network.
- Network users can communicate by email, instant messenger and voice over internet protocol (VoiP).
- Networking computers allows users to share common peripheral resources such as printers, fax machines and modems, saving money.
- Networks allow data to be transmitted to remote areas that are connected within local areas.
- Security over networks is of a high standard – users cannot see other users' files, unlike on standalone machines.
- Site (network) software licences are less expensive than buying several standalone licences.
- The cost of computing is reduced per user as compared to the development and maintenance of a group of non-networked standalone computers.
- Within networks it is much more straightforward to back up data as it is all stored on a file server.

There are also a number of disadvantages to using networks, which include:

- If a virus gets into the system it can easily spread to other computers.
- In the event of a file server breaking down, the files contained on the server become inaccessible. The client computers can still be used but are isolated.
- The cost of purchasing cabling to construct a network as well as the file servers can be high.
- The management of a large network is complicated, it requires training and a specialist network manager usually needs to be employed.
- With networks there is a risk of hacking, particularly with wide area networks. Stringent security measures, such as a firewall, are required to prevent such abuse.

Question

Describe the type of network that is suitable for 10 or more users.

How is data communicated on a network?

Any electronic communications process requires the following components:

- a source of information
- a transmitter to convert the information into data signals compatible with the communications channel
- a communications channel
- a receiver to convert the data signals back into a form the destination can understand
- the destination for the information.

The transmitter encodes the information into a suitable form to be transmitted over the communications channel. The communications channel moves this signal in the form of electromagnetic energy from the source to one or more destination receivers.

The channel may convert this energy from one form to another. This could be electrical or optical signals. It must maintain the **integrity** of the information so that the recipient can understand the message sent by the transmitter.

The communication media can be either cable or wireless. The cable may be coaxial, twisted-pair or fibre optic. The different cable types are compared in the table.

Key term

Data **integrity** is the state of data being exactly as it should be.

Coaxial	Twisted pair	Fibre optic
Electrical signal communication through the wires	Electrical signal communication through inner conductor of the wires	Optical signal communication through glass fibres
High noise contamination	Medium noise contamination	Very low noise contamination
Can be affected by external magnetic interference	Less affected by external magnetic interference	Not affected by magnetic interference
Low bandwidth	Medium bandwidth	High bandwidth
Easy installation	Reasonably easy installation	Difficult installation
Lowest cost of the three communication media	Moderately expensive compared to coaxial cable	Most expensive of the three communication media

Types of networks

Local area networks

Local area networks (LANs) are characterised by high-speed transmission over a restricted geographical area. Signals need to be boosted if the LAN is too large.

Wide area networks

While LANs operate where distances are relatively small, wide area networks (WANs) are used to link LANs that are separated by large distances ranging from a few tens of metres to thousands of kilometres.

Virtual private networks

Virtual private networks (VPNs) are a cheaper alternative to a WAN and use **dedicated** packet-switched links to interconnect two or more LANs. This creates a VPN, which interconnects several LANs by using the existing internet infrastructure.

Personal area networks

A personal area network (PAN) is a computer network organised around an individual person. PANs often involve mobile computers and smartphones.

Network topologies

Bus topology

Bus networks, which have absolutely nothing to do with the system bus of a computer, use a common backbone to connect all devices.

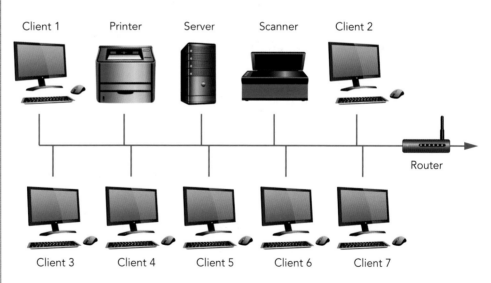

A bus network.

A single cable that functions as the backbone of the network acts as a shared communication medium that the devices connect to by way of an interface connector. When a device wishes to communicate with another network device, it transmits a broadcast message along the cable that all the devices can receive. Only the intended device actually accepts and processes the message.

Question

What is the difference between a LAN and a WAN?

Key term

Dedicated means something that is designed for one particular purpose.

Bus topologies are easy to install and require only a relatively small amount of cabling when compared to alternative topologies. Bus networks are the best choice of **topology** when the network has only a limited number of devices. If the network grows so that there are more than a few dozen computers connected to the backbone bus, then it is probable that performance will be impaired. Finally, if the backbone cable suffers a catastrophic failure, then the entire network effectively becomes unusable.

Advantages of the bus topology:

- It is easy and cheap to install as a consequence of requiring only a small quantity of cable.
- It is suitable for small networks.

Disadvantages of the bus topology:

- The cable length restricts the number of devices that can be connected to the network.
- This topology performs well only for a limited number of computers. As more devices are connected, the performance of the network becomes slower as a consequence of data collisions.

Ring topology

A network topology is referred to as a ring topology when every device has exactly two neighbours for communication purposes.

In the ring topology, all messages pass around in the same direction. This can be either clockwise or anticlockwise. As with the bus topology, should a failure in any cable occur or, in this case, a device breaks down in the ring, it can halt the entire network. Ring topologies are found in some offices and schools.

Advantages of the ring topology:

- Messages being sent between two workstations pass through all the intermediate devices, so a central server is not needed for the management of this topology.

Disadvantages of the ring topology:

- The failure of any cable within the network can cause the entire network to crash.
- Alterations, maintenance or changes being made to the network nodes can affect the performance of the whole network.

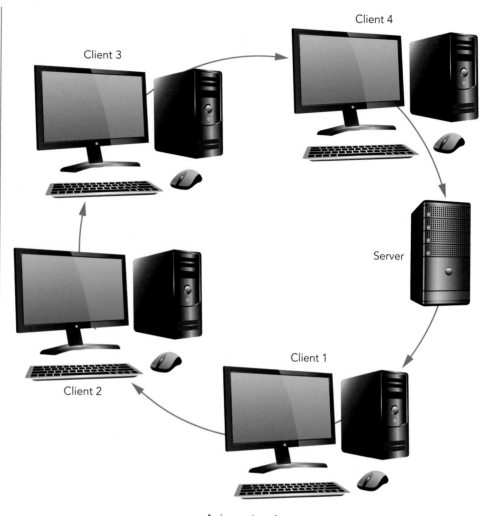

A ring network.

Star topology

The star topology is the most familiar to people as nearly all home networks use this topology. The star network has a central connection point referred to as a 'hub node', which could be a device such as a network **hub**, **switch** or router. Devices usually connect to the hub by cabling that is referred to as unshielded twisted pair (UTP) ethernet.

Star networks generally require more cable than bus topologies. However, a failure in any star network cable will only restrict access to the computer that is connected using that cable and not the entire network. If the hub fails, however, the entire network stops working.

Key terms

A **hub** is a device for connecting multiple network devices in one segment.

A **switch** is a device for connecting multiple network devices and multiple segments.

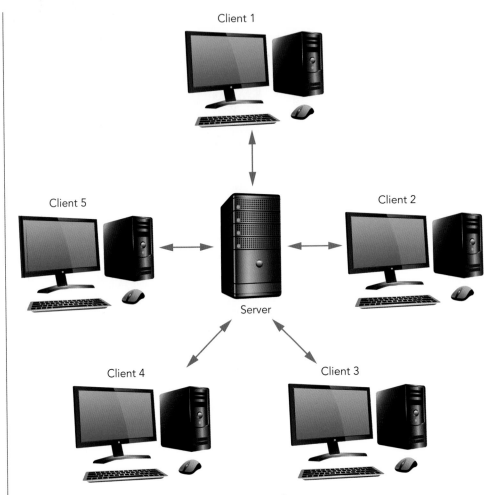

A star network.

Advantages of the star topology:

■ As a consequence of its centralised layout the topology offers operational simplicity.

■ It allows isolation of each device within the network.

Disadvantage of the star topology:

■ The network operation ultimately relies on the correct functioning of the central hub. So, if the central hub crashes it will lead to the failure of the whole network.

Wireless networks

A wireless network (WiFi) and a portable personal router (MiFi) use radio waves to communicate. Radios, mobile phones and televisions all use radio waves as well.

A computer's wireless adapter translates data into a radio signal and transmits it using an antenna, and receives radio signals and converts them into data (remember data has to be zeros and ones).

A wireless modem called a router (WiFi and MiFi) handles the two-way communication. It either receives the data from the computer's wireless adapter or receives data from the internet. In either case, it decodes the data before passing it on either to the internet server, if it is from the computer, or to the computer, if it is from the internet server. Usually the router is connected by a physical, wired ethernet or optical connection, but MiFi uses wireless networks to connect to the internet servers.

Router

A wireless network.

Websites

When you browse the internet, you join a large network and see the web pages displayed in your own browser. They are on your own computer. These pages are stored on a web server, which is not the same thing as your web browser. The web server can be located anywhere in the world; your web browser is on your own computer. The web browser interprets code that is sent to it from the web server and turns it into a web page. The code will mainly be **HTML**, but will probably also contain elements of Javascript, Flash movies and more.

You are a customer of the web server, which in computing terms is called a client.

Your computer asks for the web page and some of the code is sent back to you, the client. Most often it will just send the code, but web servers can also manipulate code within a web page before sending it to the client. To do this the web server executes a program on the server before sending the pages. The name given to this is server-side programming.

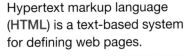

Key term

Hypertext markup language (HTML) is a text-based system for defining web pages.

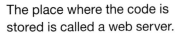

Key point

The place where the code is stored is called a web server.

The server-side program can be written in a variety of languages. Some of the programming languages and technologies that can be used are PHP, ASP (active server pages), C/C++ and JSP (Java server pages, not Javascript). There are others, but the server must support the chosen server-side language in order to work. Code executed on the web server is called server-side code. If code is executed on your browser, it is called client-side code.

Task

Think about making a booking for an aircraft flight.
- **What networks are likely to be accessed?**
- **What servers might be needed?**
- **What software would be needed?**

What is done server side?

There are a number actions that can be programmed on the server. One of the main functions that requires server-side code is to build pages customised for the type of browser that requested a page. Movies, for example, require different versions according to the browser being used. Server-side code can also draw information from a database to create information for a web page. Anything that requires information from a database, such as the number of people on the server, their address and any type of analytical information, has to be done on the server side. A visitor counter is usually a server-side program.

Modern developments in programming are blurring some aspects of client- and server-side programming. As internet speeds get faster and more reliable, items such as counters can use client-side scripting using jquery, which runs on the client side but accesses a database on the server side.

Web programmers like server-side scripts such as PHP as they are more secure than client-side code. You cannot download and steal the code if it is server side.

What is done client side?

Client-side programming is important because the client and the server are not always connected. The browser is separate from the server. By including code within the web page, a number of features can be added. This is also a much quicker way to execute code even if the client and server are connected, as the communications between parts of your computer are much faster than any internet connection.

HTML, Flash files, Javascript, ActiveX controls and a number of other technologies can be executed on the client side. You can execute any technology supported by your browser.

Security

Server-side coded scripts are much more secure than client-side scripts. Online shops have to use server-side scripting for online payments. When a user accesses his or her bank account online, the server-side script communicates with the client-side script using encryption. It would be far too insecure to use the plain text that runs on the client-side browser. Hackers would easily view the code and steal private information from the user's computer. Many web-based games run on the server side for the same reason. The programmer needs to make sure players cannot modify the data and hack into the game code.

Gaming

Flash-based games are delivered from cloud-based servers but run client side. But multi-player games and games that remember scores across players have to also be driven server side.

Most modern games use client-side detection. You carry out an action, then your system sends data packets to the game server. But this is changing, and some of the very latest games even use server-side rendering. The client browser is only used as a canvas. This enables the game designer to create 3D worlds and unique gaming experiences. But the main advantage of server-side rendering is when it is used for mobile gaming. As we discovered in earlier chapters, smartphones cannot have the large graphics processors that can be put into desktop computers. By using server-side programming the games can draw on cloud-based high-end graphics cards.

Web applications

A web application is a server-side application that can be used by accessing a web server through the internet or an intranet. The browser is used as a 'thin' client.

This type of application has become very popular as programmers are able to update and maintain web applications without end users having to update software on their own machines.

Bandwidth

Bandwidth affects the amount of data that can be transferred in a given amount of time. The quantity of information a channel can convey over a given period is determined by its ability to handle the rate of change of the signal. This is called its frequency. An analogue signal varies between a minimum and maximum frequency and the difference between those frequencies is the bandwidth of that signal. So the bandwidth of an analogue channel is the difference between the highest and lowest frequencies that can be reliably received over the channel.

Digital signals are made up of a large number of frequency components. Only those within the bandwidth of the channel can be received. It follows that the larger the bandwidth of the channel, the higher the data transfer rate can be and the more accurate the transmitted signal.

Noise

All transmission media generates some noise. As the signals pass through a communications channel the atomic particles and molecules in the transmission medium vibrate and emit random electromagnetic signals as noise. When the wanted signal is not significantly higher than the background noise, the receiver cannot separate the data from the noise and communication errors occur. Fibre-optic cable has the least noise of all the transmission media used in networks.

Data transmission nodes

Simplex

A simplex channel is unidirectional: it only allows data to flow in one direction. Television is an example of a simplex transmission. The broadcaster transmits a programme, but does not receive any signals back from your television.

Half-duplex

Half-duplex transmission allows simplex communication in both directions over a single channel. The transmitter at station A sends data to a receiver at station B. Line turnaround procedures then take place when transmission is required in the opposite direction. The station B transmitter is then enabled and communicates with the receiver at station A. The delay in the line turnaround procedures reduces the available data throughout the communications channel.

Full duplex

A full-duplex channel gives simultaneous communications in both directions but requires two channels.

Network protocols

A protocol is, in one sense, nothing more than an agreement that a particular type of data will be formatted in a particular manner. The importance of these protocols is that they provide a standard way to interact among networked computers.

Addressing

In many ways internet addressing is similar to the postal addressing system. The address on the internet is called internet protocol (IP) addressing. An IP address assigned to a host is 32 bits long and is unique.

An IP address has two parts: one part similar to the postal code and the other part similar to the house address. They are known as the net ID (netid) and the host ID (hostid).

The host is the end point of communication in the internet and where a communication starts. It could be a web server, an email server or the desktop, laptop or any computer we use for accessing the internet. The netid identifies a contiguous block of addresses.

Another popular form of address is the media access control (MAC) address. MAC addresses are six bytes (48 bits). The computer's own hardware configuration determines its MAC address. The configuration of the network it is connected to determines its IP address.

The first half of a MAC address contains the ID number of the adapter manufacturer. The second half of a MAC address represents the serial number assigned to the adapter by the manufacturer.

TCP/IP

Like any delivery system, we also need a delivery model. When you use the postal system you can ask for guaranteed delivery. On the internet, conceptual **TCP/IP** (transmission control protocol/internet protocol) is the delivery model. TCP is in charge of the reliable delivery of information, while IP is in charge of routing, using the IP addressing mechanism.

IP, however, does not worry about whether the information is delivered to the address. A key difference in the internet as opposed to the postal system is that the sending host first sends a beacon to the destination address (host) to see if it is reachable, and waits for a reply before sending the actual message. A timer is used to make sure that the message is received.

If the sending host does not hear back, it tries to send the beacon a few more times, waiting for a certain amount of time before each attempt, until it stops trying after reaching the limit on the maximum number of attempts.

When the sending host sends its beacon, it includes its source IP address. Once the connectivity is established through the beacon process, the actual transmission of the content can start.

Packets

The next issue is the size of the parcels being sent. If we have 100 large parcels to send to an address they may not fit into the Royal Mail van. We will need more than one van to deliver the parcels. The internet transfer model also operates in this fashion. Suppose that a document that we want to download from a host (web server) is 2 MB. It cannot be accommodated entirely into a single unit of IP, known as a packet, due to limitations in the underlying transmission system. This limitation is known as the maximum transmission unit (MTU). The document would need to be broken down into smaller units that fit into packets. Each packet is then labelled with both the destination and the source address, which is then routed through the internet towards the destination.

Checksum

A simple error-detection scheme is used in which each transmitted package is accompanied by a numerical value based on the number of set bits in the message. The receiving station then applies the same formula to the message and checks to make sure the accompanying numerical value is the same. If not, the receiver can assume that the message has been garbled.

Network routing and data rate

We know that packets are routed from a source to a destination. These packets may need to travel via lots of cross-points, similar to traffic intersections in a road transportation network. Cross-points in the internet are known as routers. A router's function is to read the destination address marked in an incoming IP packet, then to identify an outgoing link where the packet is to be forwarded, and to forward the packet.

Similar to the number of lanes and the speed limit on a road, a network link that connects two routers is limited by how much data it can transfer in any given amount of time. This is called the bandwidth or capacity and it is represented by a data rate, such as 1.54 megabits per second (Mbps).

Question

What is the purpose of a router on a network?

Suppose that traffic suddenly increases, for example, because many users are trying to download from the same website. The packets generated can be queued at routers or even dropped. Routers only have a limited amount of space, known as a buffer, to store backlogged packets. It is possible to reach the buffer limit. Since the basic principle of TCP/IP allows the possibility of an IP packet not being delivered, the limit of the buffer is not a problem. On the other hand, from an efficient delivery point of view, it is desirable not to have any packet lost (or at least, to minimise this).

The growing web and the internet

People often use the words internet and web interchangeably, but in reality they are fundamentally different.

Networks have been used to connect computers since the 1950s. Communication by the internet has been possible for many years, but in the early days that communication was almost exclusively accomplished via text-based email and basic file exchanges.

The world wide web (WWW or simply the web) is a relatively new idea and came along years after the internet. The web is an infrastructure of distributed information combined with software that uses networks as a vehicle to exchange that information. A web page is simply a document that contains or references various kinds of data, such as text, images, graphics, video and programs. Web pages also contain links to other web pages so that the user can move around using a point-and-click interface provided by a computer mouse. In addition to text, a web page often consists of separate elements such as images. All elements associated with a particular web page are sent to the browser when a request for that web page is made.

Web pages are created using a language called the hypertext markup language (HTML). The word hypertext refers to the fact that the information is not organised, like a book. We can embed links to other information and jump from one place to another as needed.

A website is simply a collection of related web pages, usually designed and controlled by the same person or company (although that is changing with mashups).

A few years ago groups of DJs and musicians started to make new songs by mixing two or more music tracks together. The name that they gave this was a mashup. New developments in web programming led to people starting to do the same thing. They started to use data and code from lots of external places to create something unique: to create a web mashup.

When Google Maps released some of its code as an application programming interface (API), web developers were able to integrate mapping into their own applications without developing all the code themselves. Today there are lots of video and photo hosting sites sharing part of their code with APIs, including Flickr, Yahoo and YouTube. Other APIs quickly followed with payment systems such as PayPal, Twitter, Facebook, price comparison tools for online shopping and multi-site searches.

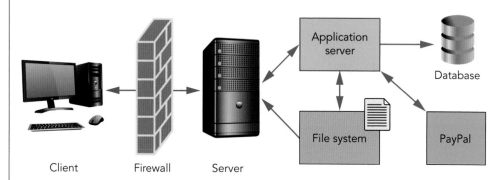

A mashup at work using PayPal's API.

Programmers were now able to integrate code from these external sources into their own code.

The internet makes the communication possible, but the web makes that communication easy, more productive and more enjoyable.

The internet, largely because of the world wide web, is now a primary vehicle for business. Electronic shopping, social networking, banking, gaming, watching the television and group management are all common online activities. The web has literally changed the way we conduct our personal and working lives.

People often talk about visiting a website as if they are physically going there. In reality the data is brought to them; they are not even visiting it virtually.

We communicate on the web using a web browser. A browser is a software tool that issues the request for the web page we want and displays it when it arrives. The requested web page data is usually stored on another computer. The computer that is set up to respond to web requests is called a web server. In a browser, we specify what web page we want using a web address. Sometimes data is delivered directly but increasingly some items appear in an iframe.

What is an iframe?

An iframe (inline frame) is an HTML tag embedded inside another HTML document on a website. An iframe is used to embed content from another source into a web page. An iframe can be configured with its own scrollbar independent of the surrounding page's scrollbar. To users, it appears as though they are still on the same site but in reality they have embedded content and programming from another source. Users do not have to reload the surrounding page.

The code for iframes often uses Javascript but iframes are designed to embed interactive applications in web pages, which could be either client or server side.

A web address

A web address is the core part of a uniform resource locator (URL), which uniquely identifies the page you want from all of the pages stored anywhere in the world. Part of a URL is the host name of the computer on which the information is stored.

Markup language

The term markup language comes from the fact that the main elements of the language take the form of tags. These are inserted into a document to annotate the information stored.

In HTML the tags indicate how the information should be displayed. HTML tags indicate the styles of a piece of data including paragraphs, images, lists and so on, as well as how it should be displayed, such as the font style, size and colour.

HTML documents are regular text and can be created in any general-purpose text editor or word processor. There are also special-purpose software tools specifically designed to help create web pages.

HTML5

HTML5 was developed around web apps, which are small, focused applications that can run on a browser or as a mobile application. HTML5 has features such as offline storage and the ability to handle data when the app is no longer connected to the internet. It also has geo-location and the ability to detect and work with the location of the user. Other improvements were designed to offer rich media support to help web designers to provide and implement audio, gaming and video elements.

Cascading style sheets

Cascading style sheets (CSS) are an extension to basic HTML that allow users to add style sheets to their web pages.

In standard HTML, to make something bold you would use the <b> tag:

```
<b>make me bold</b>
```

This works well but what if you wanted to make all the headings bold? You would have to go to every heading on the page and change the tag. But if you wanted to make the headings bold, and also change the font style and colour, you would need to add a lot of code.

With CSS, you can create a custom style elsewhere and set all its properties, give it a unique name and then simply tag your HTML to apply these stylistic properties. You can even create a separate but linked external style sheet.

Client–server model

We have looked at how a network uses a client and a server to link computers, but it is not only in networks that use cables where this model works. You may think that you are not on a network but as soon as you switch on your mobile phone or connect to the internet you are. You become a client. And client–server models don't stop there, they work within programs and even applications. If you think about a web browser, the software draws its data including words, images, video and more from the web server, which is another computer on the internet. You are a client of the web server.

With the expansion of these types of services it is very important that you understand the client–server term and how client systems work.

An explanation of the client–server model

We have seen how the client–server model is simply a term that defines the connection between two computer programs. We also know that within this model there is always one program, called a client, that requests a service or a resource from another program, called the server, which then fulfils the request.

Within any network, the client–server model is a very efficient way of connecting applications that are distributed effectively across different locations.

Computer relationships using the client–server model are very common. For example, you might want to check the details for a music concert in Birmingham. You type this into your computer and a client program in your computer sends a request to a server program at the concert venue. That program on the concert venue server will, in turn, forward the request to its own client program, which then sends a request to a database server, perhaps within another company's computer, to retrieve all the details of your requested concert. The dates, times and price of tickets are then returned back to the venue server, which then sends the information back to the client in your personal computer, which presents the information to you on your monitor.

These days, it is fair to say that almost all modern business programs use the client–server model. What is also interesting is that the internet's main program, TCP/IP, also uses this model.

There are other program relationship models in use and these include:

- **master–slave**, where one program is in charge of all other programs
- **peer to peer**, where either of the two programs is able to initiate a transaction.

Handshaking

It is a common practice when we meet someone to shake their hand as a greeting. This is true in computing as well. When two computers connect in a network they first use a handshake.

For computers to work together they have to use what are called protocols. A protocol is a set of rules that governs the transfer of data between computers. Protocols are essential for any communication between computers and networks. They determine the speed of transmission, size of bytes, error-checking methods, and even whether communication will be asynchronous or synchronous. Examples of protocols are token ring and TCP/IP. They are the method by which all networked computers set up a link through some kind of networking equipment.

Handshaking establishes what protocols to use and controls the flow of data between two or more connected computers. All network connections, such as a request from a web browser to a web server, or a file-sharing connection between peer-to-peer computers, have their own handshaking protocols, which must be completed before finishing the action requested by the user.

Key term

Peer to peer is a network arrangement where all computers are equal.

Key point

The rules or standards that control communication between devices are called protocols.

Question

What is a token?

The handshaking process usually occurs when a computer is about to communicate with what is called a foreign device to establish the rules for communication. During handshaking, the protocol parameters, which both the communicating devices and systems understand, are negotiated. As we have seen, these parameters include things such as coding issues, information transfer rate and interruption procedures.

Every communication system has five basic needs or requirements:
- a data source (this is where the data originates)
- a transmitter (a device that will be used to transmit data from its source)
- transmission media (cables or other data transfer methods)
- a receiver (a device used to receive data)
- a destination (where the data will be placed or displayed).

Transmitting the data

Any network is governed by the speed that the data can travel. If you imagine the cables, wireless connections or systems to be a motorway network, the roads have width and speed limits and can get slow if there are too many cars travelling at the same time or the motorway is full of large lorries. This is the same with networks. When discussing network protocols you will often see the word bandwidth used. Bandwidth is the amount of data which can be transmitted on a medium (cables or wireless) over a fixed period of time (over a second). It is measured using bits per second or baud. Bits per second (bps) are therefore a measure of transmission speed, the number of bits (zeros or ones) which can be transmitted in a second. The baud rate is a measure of how fast a change of state occurs (a change from a zero to a one).

Data packets

Anything sent between computers or programs has to be divided up into packets. Even a PowerPoint presentation or spreadsheet has to be divided into packets to be transmitted. Imagine an object built of Lego where each brick is a packet. Packets are small data units. Of course, once transmitted the packets have to be put back together in the correct order. In computing the open system interconnection (OSI) model looks after this. OSI is not one protocol, it is a collection of protocols. These protocols wrap each data packet with a set of instructions. The computing name for this is encapsulation. Once all the packets have been received the client needs to know they have all arrived, so the very last packet is a special one called a frame.

Here is a simple example to illustrate the handshaking process, which could involve the receiver sending a message indicating:

'I received your last message and I am ready for you to send me another one.'

A more complex handshaking scenario could involve the receiver replying with a negative acknowledgement (because the message was not received due to a crash or corruption) indicating:

'I did not receive your last message correctly, please resend it.'

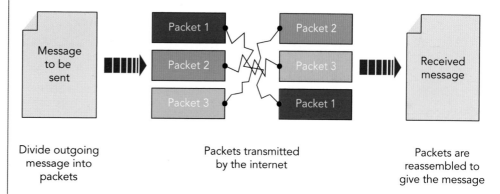

A diagrammatic representation of data packet transmission.

Differences between client-side and server-side programming

It is important to know the differences between client-side programming and server-side programming. As we have seen, client-side programming is run on the client's machine. An example of client-side programming is Javascript. Server-side programming is run on the remote server. Some examples of server-side programming languages are PHP, C# and .NET.

Topic 6
THE BIGGER PICTURE

20 Emerging trends, issues and impact

Learning outcomes

- Be aware of current and emerging trends in computing technology.
- Be aware of the impact of computing on individuals, society and the environment.
- Be aware of ethical and legal issues arising from the use of computers.
- Be aware of ownership issues relating to computing.

The importance of computer systems to the modern world

In the future, computer systems are very likely to become even more integral to our everyday lives. Think about all of the computer systems that we regularly use at the moment, such as:

- contactless payment systems that use RFID (radio frequency ID) tags in credit and debit cards that are read when a card is placed near a reader
- RFID technology in library books and in products in shops to detect if the item is being removed without payment or authorisation. This technology is also being used in clothing, where it communicates with washing machines and informs the machine how to wash the garment
- self-service supermarket checkouts that scan, weigh, process payment and give change
- the cashless catering systems that a lot of schools use
- the computers that monitor and control systems and facilities within cars
- voice-activated smartphones
- washing/drying programs on washing machines.

In business, people rely heavily on computer systems to enable them to make their jobs easier and more efficient. Computer systems allow business people to create business documentation that is error free and professional in appearance. Computer systems allow people to work together on projects. Whether they are in the next office or on opposite sides of the world, they are able to co-edit and share files easily and collaborate on the production of documentation, drawings or reports. Even calendars can be shared between colleagues so that meetings can be booked with the confidence that they don't clash with other appointments.

Key point

Computer chips control many of the products we use each day.

Task

List at least 10 everyday objects that you use each day that contain microprocessors.

With the improvements in technology, working from home has become increasingly popular. People can even securely log on to their company's network using the internet, work on files, share documents with fellow workers and use the organisation's intranet.

Banks, for example, use systems to provide:
- cashpoint machines
- online banking
- secure access to customer accounts.

Entertainment organisations use computer systems for:
- online booking services
- WiFi-connected computers and printers to issue tickets on a customer's arrival.

Schools use computer systems for:
- attendance and registration systems, sometimes even using a biometric system of registering
- cashless money systems for the dining hall
- learning environments and the storage of students' work files.

If you take a moment and think back even five years, ask yourself how much of the above technology existed then. Think about how computers have changed the way we live and the technological advances in communication, shopping, entertainment, banking, travel and even how your lessons are delivered at school.

Computer systems are now all around us and instead of being things that we use occasionally if we want to, they have now become embedded into our lives with regard to the services they provide and the data that they hold. In many ways their importance has increased so much that they are no longer just a luxury, they have become a necessity for modern living.

Task

Look at this image of a modern hospital operating room. Identify as many uses of computing microprocessors as possible.

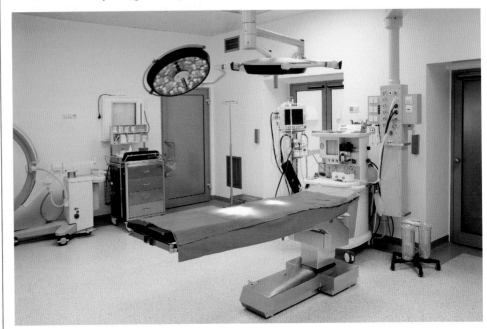

A modern operating theatre in a hospital.

Question

A patient in intensive care in a hospital is connected to various sensors. Identify some of the sensors that may be used and what they are used for.

Issues arising from the use of computers

But with all the benefits technology offers, it also brings issues. A few of them are considered here.

File sharing

The illegal sharing of music and films over the internet has become more and more of a problem as internet speeds have grown faster. Famous court cases based on intellectual property rights and privileges have hit the news.

The digital divide

Over the past few years society's dependence on computer technology has increased. The ability to communicate by email and access the internet has become an essential part of everyday life. But there are many people in the world who do not have access to the internet and this has led to a disparity called the digital divide.

This gap is of growing concern. Rural communities, low-income families, people with disabilities and areas of the developing world do not have the same advantages as more privileged households and communities.

Extension task

How would your life be different today if there were no computer systems?

Email privacy

People often write important messages in their emails. Increasingly email security has been compromised. Email was once only available to the computer literate. Today email has become a standard means of communication for millions of people. Many of these people wrongly assume that only they and the recipient of their email will be able to read the communication. This illusion of privacy is a big concern. Email travels from server to server and can be read more easily than a postcard. Recently, email privacy has become part of a debate about individual rights, corporate rights and the use of technology.

Facial recognition

Facial recognition is now used in train stations, airports and many public places. It is no longer in the realm of science fiction. But many people are concerned at the lack of security and how the captured data could be used by unscrupulous companies and individuals. Facial recognition has even found its way into social media sites.

Plagiarism

While plagiarism is not a recent problem, the internet has led to an explosion in the illegal copying of other people's work. In schools, colleges and universities tutors now have a real problem in identifying and discriminating between original work and plagiarised work.

Software piracy

With the growth of the internet, more and more people are using illegal, sometimes borrowed, software. Billions of pounds of income is lost as a result of pirated software.

Hacking

Hacking refers to trespassing or accessing data without authority. It has become more and more of a problem over the years. Sometimes the hackers unlawfully access the data, but do not damage it. But often hackers hack into data either to steal from it or to cause malicious damage. Either way, it is illegal to hack into someone else's data.

Web content

The world wide web has revolutionised communication. It is a wonderful place for information exchange and self-expression. Anyone can gain an extensive global audience. But in recent years this has led to a rapid growth in everything from pornographic material to instructions for making bombs, hate propaganda and web fraud.

Invasion of privacy

The chances are that the more you use the internet, the easier it is for someone to invade your privacy. Your data is probably stored around the world in a wide range of databases. Your activity and life are probably being monitored. And it is not just the internet where this is a problem. Some people use a store's loyalty card when shopping; their details and what they are purchased will be recorded on the store's computers. Critics of the system will argue that these loyalty cards compromise the privacy of customers, but the retailers who use them argue that they are a way of offering special offers targeted to the right customers.

Computer viruses

It is estimated that over £10 million of damage can result from a single computer virus. With so many viruses appearing, the issue of computer viruses is a growing problem.

Encryption

Encryption is necessary when someone enters personal information or banking information on the internet to make a purchase. But encryption can be of use to a terrorist. It allows them to send secret messages that the security service cannot interpret. Even the information that you enter through an encrypted connection could be accessible at the other end by a criminal.

Deep linking

Users of the world wide web frequently move from page to page following **hyperlinks** which can appear as images or text. Often the hyperlink takes users away from the website they are on, moving them to another website. Originally, hyperlinks were at the heart of the web. Deep linking occurs when one web page includes a hyperlink to a web page that is buried deep within another site. This can give the appearance that the

Question

Explain the term encryption.

Key term

A hyperlink is an item on a web page that directs the user to another location when clicked.

hyperlinked pages are part of the original website. A growing number of companies are concerned that these steal their content.

Online gambling

Online gambling is becoming a real problem in the Western world. The internet opens up opportunities to lose vast amounts of money while staying in the comfort of one's own home.

Cybersquatting

Cybersquatting is when someone purchases a **domain name** knowing that it will be useful to a well-known company. They then sit on the name until they can sell it at a higher price. Often companies with well-known trademarks are unable to purchase a domain for their name as it is owned by a cybersquatter. Common names are also subject to cybersquatting.

Cookies

Internet cookies are very small text files that are downloaded from a web server to a web browser. They record the activity on the browser, and then send it back to the server. While cookies can be very useful for auto-compiling forms, they can also be used by advertisers and less scrupulous users.

Unlicensed computer professionals

Plumbers, electricians, doctors and many people who provide a service to the public are often licensed. Computer professionals are not. This makes it almost impossible to know whether the person who is fixing your computer is both competent and reliable. Remember that people accessing your computer have full access to all of the data on it.

Downloadable components

More cases are appearing in the news where children start to play a free game and then download extra characters and plug-ins, not realising that these are all chargeable additions. The use of a free game followed by purchasable components is a growing issue, particularly with smartphone and tablet use.

The need for reliability in modern computer systems

As we have discussed earlier, in these modern technological times we have come to depend on computer systems a great deal, taking advantage of the services that they offer and the data that they can store. You can therefore understand that excellent reliability in computer systems is very important.

Key term

A domain name is a human readable name for a resource location on a network. It is changed to a numerical IP address by the DNS server.

Task

Why do all devices using computers, for example, washing machines, DVD players and televisions have both ROM and RAM?

What is reliability?

When someone can be depended on to do something we want them to do, we call them reliable. Computer systems are similar. However, the advantage with computer systems is that reliability can be measured.

Key term

A metric is a measurement of something's performance. Not to be confused with metric units of measurement!

Systems administrators have the responsibility for the reliability of an organisation's computer system and this is measured by an average **metric** of some kind. The following are some common metrics used to judge the reliability of computer systems:

- AVAIL: this uses the percentage of time that a system is available to users but ignores any planned maintenance periods when the system is down.
- MTTF: stands for 'mean time to failure' and is the average number of hours that a system operates before it goes wrong. This metric tends to be most commonly applied to hardware, for example servers.

The consequences of failure

Computer system failures can be catastrophic for both organisations and for people. Just imagine that your computer's hard disk failed right at this moment. What effect would this have on you? What if it held all of your GCSE work for every subject or your whole music collection? You have some sort of backup system just in case this happens, don't you?

What if an organisation that provides telephone and broadband services had a fire in its data centre and the equipment holding all of their customer accounts went up in flames. It makes sense for the company to have in place plans and strategies for disaster recovery.

Question

Explain three instances in everyday objects that you personally use where time between failures could be critical.

Redundancy

It is a fact of life that systems will break down eventually and so there is a need to put strategies in place to deal with this. With regard to computer systems the method that is used is called redundancy.

Redundancy is a method of breakdown prevention where important parts of a system are duplicated so that in the event of a failure the other components can take its place.

Data redundancy

Data redundancy is a strategy where important data is duplicated in a number of places within the computer system. This is so that if one area of the system breaks down or becomes corrupted, the data will not be lost. An example of this is running two hard disk drives in parallel, where they both store the same data.

Software redundancy

Software redundancy is a less common strategy that tends to be used for safety-critical applications. The reason for software redundancy is that it is very difficult to create programs that don't contain any bugs at all and, in the event of a bizarre fault, an undetected bug may have disastrous consequences.

For critical software where failure cannot be allowed to happen, there will be three software routines in place, each written by independent programming teams, each producing the same output when the same input is applied. These systems tend to be in place in areas such as:

- aircraft
- medical equipment
- railway safety controls
- nuclear power stations.

Backing up

As well as redundancy, organisations use a strategy where data is stored in other locations. This method is called backing up of data.

For people who perhaps run a small office, it is important to attach an external hard drive and a good backup program on each personal computer they use.

For organisations using network servers, the common practice is to use digital tape machines to replicate data on a remote server. Large organisations may even duplicate a whole data centre in a separate location so that in the event of a fire no data will be lost. Recently, individuals and organisations have begun to contract external companies who specialise in data storage. The businesses and individuals upload their data to a remote data centre, which is maintained and managed by the specialist company.

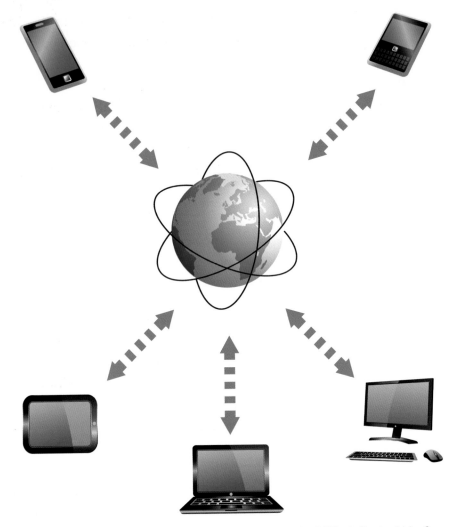

Backing up using the internet. Why is this a good idea? Why is it a bad idea?

Key term

Any software, hardware or storage running on the internet can be called cloud computing. In cloud computing you use the software on machines in the cloud instead of using your own personal computer to carry out or store your work.

This is part of the **cloud computing** system that is increasing in popularity as a cost-effective backup solution for businesses and individuals. Some modern software even backs up the data to remote cloud-based servers automatically, sometimes every few seconds. But cloud computing offers more than just backing up and shared documents. Cloud computing lets users access all their applications and documents from anywhere in the world.

Question

List five criteria that you would need to consider in developing a policy for backing up your data.

Cloud computing has led to a major change in how we back up data, store information and run applications. Instead of installing applications (often referred to as apps) on individual computers, everything can be hosted in the cloud. But as with everything in computing there are advantages and disadvantages with cloud computing.

Cloud computing

Cloud computing has many advantages. These include the following:

- *Lower computer or device costs.* Users do not need an expensive computer to run cloud computing's web-based applications. Applications run in the cloud so they do not need the processing power or hard disk space that you would need for locally installed software. Your computing device requires a smaller hard disk and less memory. This has helped to enable the growth in mobile devices with small solid-state hardware.
- *Improved performance.* With fewer programs using the computer's memory, users get better performance from their computing systems.
- *Reduced software costs.* Instead of purchasing expensive software applications you can get most of what you need online at a much lower cost or even for free.
- *Instant software updates.* Cloud-based software is always up to date.
- *Improved compatibility.* You don't have to worry about the documents you create on your machine being compatible with your other devices. There are no format incompatibilities when everyone is sharing documents and apps in the cloud.
- *Unlimited storage capacity.* Cloud computing offers limitless storage.
- *Automatic backup.* A hard disk crash on a computer can destroy all your valuable data but if it is in the cloud a computer crash shouldn't affect any of your data.
- *Universal access.* You don't carry your files and documents with you on the cloud. They stay in the cloud, and you access them whenever you have a computer or mobile device and an internet connection. All your documents are instantly available wherever you are.
- *Device independence.* The user is not limited to working on a document stored on a single computer or network. You can change computer and even change to your mobile device, and the documents follow you through the cloud.

Cloud computing does have several disadvantages. These include the following:

- *Cloud computing requires a reliable internet connection.* Cloud computing is impossible if you can't connect to the internet.
- *Cloud computing will not work as well with low-speed connections.* Web-based apps and large documents and images require a lot of bandwidth.

- *Can be slower.* Even on a very fast connection, web-based applications can sometimes be slower than accessing a similar software program on a desktop or laptop computer.
- *Limited features.* Many web-based applications do not have as many features as conventional computer programs, but this is changing and some new apps have enhanced features.
- *Security.* As all your data is stored on the cloud, it is more vulnerable.

Given the many advantages, Apple, Google and Microsoft have all developed cloud-based software and data services.

Cloud computing: do you think that this will mean the end of desktop storage of data?

Question

Describe the benefits and drawbacks to a rural school in moving to a cloud-computing model.

A growing number of people want to access the latest version of their documents on a range of devices, but the benefit of shared documents in businesses where a number of people work together on a single project is driving this cloud-based technology forward even faster. This has also led to changes in computer programming, with web-based computer languages such as PHP, HTML5 and Java becoming more and more popular.

Question

What are the implications of cloud computing to computer programmers?

Developments in computing technology

Quantum computing

Quantum computing is based on quantum physics. It takes advantage of the properties of atoms or nuclei that allow them to work together.

Rather than storing information as zeros or ones as conventional computers do, a quantum computer uses what are called qubits, short for quantum bits. These can be a one or a zero or even both at the same time. Because of this, qubits do not rely on the traditional binary nature of computing. While traditional computers encode information into bits using binary numbers and can only do calculations on one set of numbers at once, quantum computers use spinning photons that might represent a one or a zero, might represent a combination of the two or might represent a number expressing that the state of the qubit is somewhere between one and zero, or even many different numbers at once. It also has some ability to produce interference between various different numbers.

By doing a computation on many different numbers at once, a quantum computer has the potential to be much more powerful than a conventional computer of the same size. However, quantum computing is not as good as a conventional computer for tasks such as word processing and email; it is better suited to complex computer modelling and indexing very large databases.

Advantages of quantum computing include the following:
- It is faster than conventional computers.
- It is much more powerful than conventional computers.
- It is smaller than conventional computers.

Disadvantages of quantum computing include the following:
- It is hard to control quantum particles.
- It is much more expensive than conventional computers.
- It is very difficult to build compared to conventional computers.
- Lots of heat is generated in quantum computing.

DNA computing

DNA computing does not use traditional silicon-based computer technologies. It is a form of computing that uses DNA, biochemistry and molecular biology. DNA computing is also called bimolecular computing.

The main benefit of using DNA computers is that they can solve many complex problems at the same time. This is known as parallel processing.

As it is possible to fit more than 10 trillion DNA molecules into an area less than 1 cm^3, a DNA computer could hold 10 terabytes of data and parallel process 10 trillion calculations all at the same time.

Advantages of DNA computing include the following:
- It is extremely fast compared to conventional computers in complex modelling.
- It is very light in weight compared to conventional computers.
- The amount of power required is much less than a conventional computer.

Disadvantages of DNA computing include the following:
- Errors are more common due to the complexity of DNA strands.
- It is much more expensive than conventional computers.
- It is very difficult to build compared to conventional computers.
- Problems that need a sort algorithm are slower than on a conventional computer.
- Simple problems actually take longer to process.

Nanotechnology

Nanotechnology, sometimes called nanotech, is the manipulation of matter on an atomic, molecular and supramolecular scale. It is used to make very small macro-scale products. Nanotech products often have at least one dimension sized from 1 to 100 nanometres.

Many governments have invested a great deal of money into nanotechnology research as the field of potential uses is very wide. Areas where nanotechnology could be used include surface science, organic chemistry, molecular biology and semiconductor physics. The use of nanotechnology in semiconductors makes this an area of research important to anyone studying computer science.

The silicon transistors in your computer may be replaced in 10 years' time by transistors based on carbon nanotubes. This will make them smaller and much faster.

Advantages of nanotechnology include the following:
- It is much faster than conventional silicon components.
- It is much smaller than conventional silicon components.

Disadvantages of nanotechnology include the following:

- Atomic weapons could be more accessible and be made to be more powerful and more destructive with nanotechnology.
- It is very expensive and difficult to manufacture, which is probably why products made with nanotechnology are more expensive.
- Since the particles are very small, respiratory problems can arise from breathing them in.

Artificial intelligence

Artificial intelligence is the branch of computer science concerned with making computers behave and act like humans.

At present there are no computers that are able to simulate human behaviour completely. But in the field of games, the best computer chess programs are now capable of beating humans. In the area of robotics, computers are used in a large number of assembly plants, but they are capable only of very limited tasks.

Natural-language processing is, however, a big growth area as it allows people to interact with computers without needing any specialised knowledge. You can simply talk to the computer.

Many expert systems help human experts in fields such as medicine and engineering, but they are very expensive to produce and are helpful only in special situations.

There are a number of programming languages that are used almost exclusively for artificial intelligence applications. The two most common ones are Prolog and LISP.

Glossary

Acceptance testing   Acceptance testing is a validation test that is carried out to judge whether requirements of a specific criterion or a whole contract have been successfully achieved.

Address   The address is a location in main memory used to store data or instructions.

Algorithm   An algorithm is simply a set of steps that defines how a task is performed.

ALU   The arithmetic logic unit (ALU) performs all the arithmetic and logical operations within the CPU.

Application software   Application software consists of programs that perform specific tasks.

Application testing   Application testing usually (but not always) involves executing an application with the purpose of finding errors or bugs within the software.

Architecture   The internal, logical structure and organisation of computer hardware is called the architecture.

Assembly language   Assembly language is a low-level programming language. It uses mnemonic codes and labels to represent machine-level code. Each instruction corresponds to just one machine operation.

Beta testing   Beta testing follows alpha testing and is an acceptance testing by external users.

Binary tree   A binary tree is a data structure of nodes or junctions that is constructed in a hierarchy.

Boolean   Boolean is a value that can only be true or false.

Buffering   Buffering is a temporary storage area, usually but not always in RAM. The main purpose of buffers is to act as a holding area, enabling the computer to manipulate data before transferring it to a device.

Bus   The bus is a part of a computer's architecture that transfers data and signals between all the components of the computer.

Cache   Cache memory is special high-speed memory used by a computer.

Central processing unit   The central processing unit (CPU) of the computer contains the control unit, arithmetic logic unit and cache memory. A CPU is a type of processor that runs the system. The name processor is a more generic term but is often used to mean the same thing. The problem with using the term processor when referring to the CPU is that there will be other processors in a computing system but only one CPU.

Cipher   A cipher is where letters in words are rearranged to hide the original words.

Client   The client requests services from a server.

Cloud computing   Any software, hardware or storage running on the internet can be called cloud computing. In cloud computing you use the software on machines in the cloud instead of using your own personal computer to carry out or store your work.

Colour depth   Colour depth (or bit depth) refers to the number of bits used for each pixel or dot. The more bits there are, the more colours can be represented.

Comparison   Comparison refers to comparing the values of two items and returning either true or false.

Compiler   A compiler is a piece of translation software that converts high-level source code into machine (object) code.

Concurrently   Concurrently means happening at the same time as something else.

Constants   Constants store values, but as the name implies, those values remain constant throughout the execution of an application.

Control unit   The control unit works with the CPU to control the flow of data within a computer system.

Cryptographic   Cryptographic means the technique of writing or solving codes.

Data compression   Data compression is the reduction in file size to reduce download times and storage requirements.

Data persistence   Data persistence is the ability of programs to save data and return to it and reload that data when the program is run again.

Data redundancy   Data redundancy is the unnecessary repetition or duplication of data.

Debugger   A debugger is a piece of software that helps a programmer to track down faults in a program.

Debugging   The process of testing a program for errors during its execution is a cyclic activity called debugging.

Decision symbol   A decision symbol always makes a Boolean choice.

Decomposition   Decomposition is a general approach to solving a problem by breaking it up into smaller problems then solving it one problem at a time.

Dedicated   Dedicated means something that is designed for one particular purpose.

Do-while statements   Do-while statements are efficient loops that will continue to loop until the condition is false.

Domain name   A domain name is a human readable name for a resource location on a network. It is changed to a numerical IP address by the DNS server.

Embedded   Embedded systems usually form part of an electronic device. They are the lowest level of an operating system that controls the hardware.

Encrypt and decipher   Encrypt and decipher means to convert into a code and convert back from code.

Field   The smallest item or characteristic of something stored in a database is called a field.

Flash memory   Flash memory is solid-state memory used as secondary storage in portable devices and is also used as removable memory in things like USB drives.

Flat file database   A database consisting of only one table is called a flat file database.

High-level programming languages   High-level programming languages are languages that resemble a natural language. Each instruction translates into many machine instructions.

HTML   Hypertext markup language (HTML) is a text-based system for defining web pages.

Hub   A hub is a device for connecting multiple network devices in one segment.

Hyperlink   A hyperlink is an item on a web page that directs the user to another location when clicked.

Integer   An integer is a whole number, positive or negative, with no decimal or fractional part.

Integrity   Data integrity is the state of data being exactly as it should be.

Interactive device   An interactive device has an input process and an output process.

IP address   The IP (internet protocol) address is a number that identifies a device on a TCP/IP network.

Iteration   Iteration or repetition is when a group of instructions is executed repeatedly until a condition is met (a loop).

Linked list   A linked list is a data structure that makes it easy to rearrange data without having to move data in memory.

Machine code   Machine code is the instruction in binary used by the CPU.

Magnetic hard disk   A magnetic hard disk is a secondary storage device using magnetised platters to store data and files.

Metric   A metric is a measurement of something's performance. Not to be confused with metric units of measurement!

Modularity   Modularity is breaking a task down into smaller modules.

Motherboard   The motherboard is a central printed circuit board that holds all the crucial hardware components of the system and enables them to work together.

Nested loops   Nested loops have an outer loop and one or more inner loops. Each time the outer loop repeats, the inner loops are re-entered and start again as if new.

Nesting   Nesting is adding structures inside other structures.

Operating system   An operating system is the software that controls all of the computer's hardware. It acts as an interface between the user and the hardware and also between applications and the hardware.

Optical drive   An optical drive is a secondary storage device that uses lasers to read (and write) data to a reflective surface. It is sometimes used for storing files to be distributed or transferred or for backup of important files, but other forms of backup are now becoming more popular.

Overflow   When a number becomes too large to fit into the number of bits allocated it is said to overflow and some bits are 'lost', leaving an incorrect value.

Parallel algorithms   Parallel algorithms are used with computers running parallel processors.

Peer to peer   Peer to peer is a network arrangement where all computers are equal.

Print   It's important to know that when we have print in a piece of code we don't actually mean output it on a sheet of paper. The code never actually prints anything, it just displays it on your screen.

Procedure scope   Procedure scope is when a variable can be read and modified only from within the procedure in which it is declared.

Program counter   The program counter is simply a register in the CPU that keeps the address of the next instruction.

Pseudocode   Pseudocode is an easy-to-read language to help with the development of coded solutions.

RAM   RAM (random access memory) is the main memory of a computer used to store data, applications and the operating system while it is in use. When the power is turned off, RAM loses its data.

Real   A real number can have decimal or fractional parts.

Record   A record is all the data about one item in a database.

ROM   ROM (read-only memory) is a store for data in a computer that cannot be overwritten. Data in ROM is always available and is not lost when the computer is turned off.

Secondary storage   Secondary storage is non-volatile storage used to store programs and files that need to be kept even when a computer's power is not on.

Sensor   A sensor is a device that can detect physical conditions, for example, temperature, weight, light and sound.

Sequence   A sequence is where a set of instructions or actions is ordered, meaning that each action follows the previous action.

Sequence process   The sequence process is just a series of processes that operate one after the other, *if–then–else*.

Sequence, selection and looping   Sequence, selection and looping are three fundamental control structures used in programming.

Serial algorithms   Serial algorithms are where each step or operation is carried out in a linear order.

Server   A server provides services to a client.

String   A string may contain zero or more characters, including letters, digits, special characters and blanks.

Subprogram   A subprogram is a computer program contained within another program. It operates semi-independently of the main program.

Switch   A switch is a device for connecting multiple network devices and multiple segments.

TCP/IP   TCP/IP is a transmission control protocol/internet protocol consisting of a set of standards that control how data is sent across networks including the internet.

Test plans   Test plans describe how each phase or level of testing of an application is to be done.

Topology   A network topology is simply the arrangement of devices on a computer network.

Trace table   A trace table is a method of using data to check that a flowchart or code covers all possibilities correctly.

Translator   A translator is a program to convert high-level or assembly-level commands into machine code.

Truth table   A truth table is a method for recording all the possible input combinations and determining the output for each when using logic gates.

User interface   A user interface is the access point and the boundary between the computer and the user.

Validation   Validation is the process of checking data as it is input to ensure that it is reasonable.

Variable   A variable can be assigned different values during a program's execution.

Virtual memory   Virtual memory is a section of the hard disk used as if it were RAM to supplement the amount of main memory available to the computer.

Volatile memory   Volatile memory cannot store data when the computing device is turned off. Non-volatile memory can.

While statements   While statements are efficient loops that will continue to loop until the condition is false.

Index